Understanding **Human Sexual Inadequacy**

This is an explanation of Masters and Johnson's research and patient care studies. Written in an easy-to-understand language, it is the only analysis authorized by Masters and Johnson.

"A conservative estimate would indicate half the marriages [in this country] as either presently sexually dysfunctional or imminently so in the future."
—Masters and Johnson
Human Sexual Inadequacy

About **Human Sexual Inadequacy**

"A valuable book which tells how the authors have helped many . . . impotent or non-orgasmic or insensitive men and women who in the past we doctors have often turned away as therapeutically hopeless. The writers always treat two sexual partners at the same time and try more to bring about a happy marriage than just a cured man."
—Walter C. Alvarez, M.D.
Modern Medicine

UNDERSTANDING HUMAN SEXUAL INADEQUACY

by
Fred Belliveau
and
Lin Richter

A NATIONAL GENERAL COMPANY

UNDERSTANDING HUMAN SEXUAL INADEQUACY
*A Bantam Book / published by arrangement with
Little, Brown and Company*

Bantam edition published July 1970

Back cover photograph courtesy Linda Woodford

*All rights reserved.
Copyright © 1970 by Fred Belliveau and Lin Richter.
This book may not be reproduced in whole or in part, by
mimeograph or any other means, without permission.
For information address: Little, Brown and Company,
34 Beacon Street, Boston, Massachusetts 02106.*

Published simultaneously in the United States and Canada

---

*Bantam Books are published by Bantam Books, Inc., a National
General company. Its trade-mark, consisting of the words "Bantam
Books" and the portrayal of a bantam, is registered in the United
States Patent Office and in other countries. Marca Registrada.
Bantam Books, Inc., 666 Fifth Avenue, New York, N.Y. 10019.*

PRINTED IN THE UNITED STATES OF AMERICA

to
the memory of
Arthur H. Thornhill, Sr.

Foreword

This book brings reassurance to the great number of people in this country who suffer from sexual dysfunction. Written clearly in nontechnical language, it supplies information which reflects established sexual fact rather than myth or misconception. It should help many people to achieve a new level of understanding about sex and to lead happier lives.

Fred Belliveau has been our editor at Little, Brown for *Human Sexual Response* and *Human Sexual Inadequacy*. Through the years we have depended upon his tastefulness and judgment in the preparation and dissemination of our research in book format. Since various journalists have written about our work for the general reader in the past, we suggested to Mr. Belliveau that he would be an appropriate person to present an explanation of the findings of our second text, *Human Sexual Inadequacy*.

Lin Richter, his co-author, is editor in the Medical Book Division at Little, Brown. Their knowledge of our professional philosophy and our work together, with their experience in the medical field, has enabled them to write an accurate and perceptive account of our work. In a field that is filled with written half-truths, this is welcome.

Their dual approach carries through an important concept of our own. If a dual-sex therapy team treats couples for sexual dysfunction, then it is appropriate that a man and woman writing team explain how couples are helped to overcome their sexual difficulties.

WILLIAM H. MASTERS
VIRGINIA E. JOHNSON

Authors' Note

When *Human Sexual Response* was published in 1966, it was intended for a scientific audience. Since so many general readers were interested in its contents there was a need to translate it into simpler words than appear in the original text. Ruth and Edward Brecher performed this job admirably in their book, *An Analysis of Human Sexual Response.** Masters and Johnson's second book, *Human Sexual Inadequacy,* published in April, 1970, is also technical and directed primarily to a professional audience. Once again it is important to interpret the new information Masters and Johnson have made available and to present it in ordinary language so that nonprofessional people can read it more easily. This is what we have attempted to do.

We hope that both the original book and our interpretation will offer understanding and insight to people with sexual dysfunction.

In *Understanding Human Sexual Inadequacy* we have reported all of Masters and Johnson's work to date, in chronological fashion, offering their comments and ours. We have provided background information about them to give readers a sense of their personalities and how they started their investigation in this neglected field. There is a description of their early laboratory

---

* *An Analysis of Human Sexual Response,* edited by Ruth and Edward Brecher (Boston: Little, Brown, 1966).

work, which led to the publication of *Human Sexual Response*, a brief synopsis of which appears in Chapter 5.

Emphasis in this book is on Masters and Johnson's second volume dealing with sexual inadequacy. In it, the authors tell specifically, for the first time, how they help men and women overcome the problems which prevent them from enjoying sex. We have tried to explain their therapy principles and techniques in detail.

We express our special gratitude to William Masters and Virginia Johnson, respectively Director and Assistant Director of the Reproductive Biology Research Foundation, St. Louis, for their cooperation and endorsement of this project.

We are also especially indebted to Judith Kennedy, George McKinnon, and Howard Richter, M.D., for the many suggestions they offered which improved the manuscript. Robert Demarest, one of America's best medical illustrators, kindly consented to prepare our drawings, which were redrawn, or modified, from *Human Sexual Response* and *Human Sexual Inadequacy*. We are proud to have his work included.

For years, as medical editors, we have advised our physician authors how to prepare material for publication. In our turn-about role as first-time authors, we owe a special debt to our editors, J. Randall Williams and Eliot Fremont-Smith of Little, Brown, and to Marc Jaffe of Bantam Books.

Several colleagues worked after hours for us typing the manuscript and doing other essential jobs. For their help we want to thank Cynthia Barahona, Barbara Davis, Karen and Bill Decker, Judith Haigh, Nancy Holbrook, Lenore Klein, Joan McClure, and Peter Mitchell.

Finally we want to thank our families for their forbearance, their encouragement, and their support.

F. B.
L. R.

Contents

Foreword, by William H. Masters
and Virginia E. Johnson   vii
Authors' Note   ix

PART I: THE NEED TO KNOW

1. The Sex Helpers   3
2. What Are They Like?   10
3. How They Started   18
4. Volunteers in the Laboratory:
   Who, How and Why   25
5. *Human Sexual Response:*
   The First Masters and Johnson Report   32
6. After Publication of *Human Sexual Response*   58

PART II: UNDERSTANDING HUMAN SEXUAL INADEQUACY

7. Rapid Treatment of Human Sexual Inadequacy:
   Principles of the Program   71
8. Rapid Treatment of Human Sexual Inadequacy:
   The Daily Program   87
9. Premature Ejaculation   111

10. Ejaculatory Incompetence	124
11. Primary and Secondary Impotence	130
12. Replacement Partners and Partner Surrogates	150
13. Orgasmic Dysfunction in Women	157
14. Vaginismus	184
15. Painful Intercourse	195
16. Sex in the Aging	207
17. Doctors and Other Therapists: Do They Always Help?	217
18. Statistics of the Treatment Program	225

PART III: EPILOGUE

An interview with Dr. Masters and Mrs. Johnson about their present and future work   233

UNDERSTANDING HUMAN SEXUAL INADEQUACY

PART I
THE NEED TO KNOW

CHAPTER 1

The Sex Helpers

A vast number of people need help for their sexual inadequacies. For years Dr. William H. Masters and Mrs. Virginia E. Johnson, sex researchers and directors of the Reproductive Biology Research Foundation in St. Louis, have received hundreds of "distress" letters every week from men and women who ask for assistance with their sex problems. For every troubled person who writes a letter, there are obviously many more who do not. "A conservative estimate," write Masters and Johnson in *Human Sexual Inadequacy,* "would indicate half the marriages [in this country] as either presently sexually dysfunctional or imminently so in the future."

What makes men impotent even when they have an attractive and loving partner, or women unable to reach orgasm even when sexually involved with a romantic man who really cares? Today, these difficulties, which have concerned men and women since ancient times, can usually be overcome. A new treatment program has been developed, and its rate of success is both impressive and enormously encouraging. Masters and Johnson find that the average troubled couple stands statistically a seventy-five to eighty percent chance of having their dysfunction reversed in only two weeks of therapy at the Foundation. As a result of their laboratory findings and experience with patients, Masters and Johnson are learning what goes wrong with sex in marriage. The potential to ease human suffering which their pioneering efforts offer may be more important for our age than any miracle drug.

Sexologists Before Masters and Johnson

Masters and Johnson take their place in a line of distinguished scientists in Western culture who have, from Victorian times to the present, studied human sexuality, and who have tried to make the role of sex in our lives more clearly understood.[1] The early researchers were strongly influenced by the restrictive patterns of Victorian thinking, especially in their own childhoods, yet each was able to push significantly beyond these restrictive patterns to make his individual contribution to the study of human sexuality.

Havelock Ellis (1859-1939), an English physician, was the first of the Victorians to impart a tone of modernity to sexual attitudes. In his scholarly series, *Studies in the Psychology of Sex,* published between 1896 and 1928, Ellis argued that attitudes toward sex are individual and culturally determined This was a great departure from centuries of thinking that claimed human sexuality to be the same in all people, and it is a keystone of all modern research in sexual psychology.

The contributions of Sigmund Freud (1856-1939)

---

[1] An excellent account of their lives and contributions is in Edward Brecher's book, *The Sex Researchers* (Boston: Little, Brown, 1969; paperback ed., New York: Bantam Books).

are known to most readers. He named the unconscious, explored its relationship to conscious behavior, labeled sexual components of personality and invented the therapy process of psychoanalysis. Freud was one of the first physicians who listened to patients with sexual (and other) difficulties and attempted to interpret such difficulties therapeutically in the context of their lives. He was the first to assert the importance of insight as a requisite for cure of emotional problems. Freud taught a host of followers, many of whom adhered rigidly to his theories, and some of whom branched out to establish their own "schools" of psychoanalysis. Today, many of Freud's theories have been discarded or modified or added to, but his impact on the modern age and on both imaginative and scientific thinking is second to none.

Theodor Hendrik van de Velde (1873-1937), a Dutch gynecologist, also made an important contribution to sexology. His book, *Ideal Marriage,* published in 1926, has sold over a million copies and is the most famous of all marriage manuals. In it he stressed that sex was not the evil much of Victorian society believed it to be. He also concentrated in his writings on the importance of the man and woman together in a sexual relationship—on the joys of giving and receiving sexual pleasure rather than just considering the sexual attitude or satisfaction of one partner—a concept Masters and Johnson revived and modified in their own studies. Most would now agree that much of van de Velde's *Ideal Marriage* sounds slightly old-fashioned. It was, however, the first marriage manual to interweave what was known about sex physiology with a large dose of romance. Unfortunately, he took away an element of naturalness in sexual functioning for people who followed his instructions literally because of his commitment to the simultaneous orgasm as the ultimate in sexual expression. This undoubtedly frustrated generations of couples who were not able to achieve it. Van de Velde is also the prime target of critics like Masters and Johnson who feel that marriage manuals in general, and especially *Ideal Marriage,* have spread inaccurate information and given poor guidance on many subjects—as, for instance, the still prevalent but erroneous notion that the male should concentrate steadfastly on direct manipulation of the clitoris to achieve female arousal.

The first great figure in the study of human sexology in the United States was Robert Latou Dickinson (1861-1950), also a gynecologist. His three books and numerous articles and his many years as an effective teacher made the scientific study of sex acceptable in this country. *A Thousand Marriages,* written with L. Beam (1931), *The Single Woman* (1934), and *Atlas of Human Sex Anatomy* (1933), were all landmark contributions. Dickinson was among the earliest investigators to record statistics about female sexual habits from gynecologic patients, and to look at patients in order to learn more about internal female anatomy. For example, he examined the vaginas of women using a glass tube resembling a penis through which light could shine, thus allowing direct observation of the vaginal interior. This was a precursor of the more sophisticated plastic phallus developed later by Masters and Johnson to study the responses of women who were sexually stimulated. Many of the present-day leaders in sex research and marriage counseling were trained by Dickinson. He had a long and active life, and when he was in his eighties he served as a consultant to Alfred Kinsey.

Alfred C. Kinsey (1894-1956), a zoologist by training, founded the Institute for Sex Research at Bloomington, Indiana, in 1938. In *Sexual Behavior in the Human Male* (1948) and *Sexual Behavior in the Human Female* (1953), Kinsey and his associates studied human sexuality quantitatively for the first time. Previous researchers had reported small statistical studies—and, of course, case histories of *abnormal* behavior were plentiful—but no one had ever studied representative sexual activities of such a large sampling of people. The Kinsey interview became legend, and many later sex researchers took valuable pointers from it. Kinsey's volunteers were not a scientifically picked population sample; consequently, his findings probably could not accurately reflect the sexual behavior of a cross-section of the population. Nevertheless, Kinsey made an enormous contribution; more than any other person he made the study of normal sex behavior acceptable.

Masters and Johnson's Major Contributions

Supplying Facts. For centuries there has been a paucity of accurate information about sex, even taking into account the knowledge given us by the post-Victorian sexologists. Few real facts about how our bodies respond during sexual functioning were known before Masters and Johnson began their eleven-year study in 1954. All other areas and systems of the body had been studied in detail by medical scientists, however, the physiology of human sexual response remained a "last frontier." Masters and Johnson's initial research resulted in the publication of their first book, *Human Sexual Response,* which presented their findings after observing natural sexual activity in the laboratory.

Two-week Rapid Therapy Program. Masters and

Johnson's second book, *Human Sexual Inadequacy*, published in April, 1970, reports their clinical findings from their eleven-year study of sexual dysfunction begun in 1958. The two-week therapy program was developed during this study. Having a couple work daily in an intensive psychotherapeutic program for removal of symptoms of sexual inadequacy had never been done before.

Dual-sex Therapy Team. Dr. Masters discovered, when he began his laboratory work, that he needed assistance in evaluating female responses from a female point of view. When Mrs. Johnson, who joined him in 1957, proved extremely effective in this role, they continued the team concept in their therapy program. The dual-sex therapy team is one of the most innovative treatment concepts; they feel that a man and woman working together can achieve much better results than either working alone.

Aging and Sex. Masters and Johnson's experience in the laboratory and with patients showed them that most people had extremely inaccurate ideas about older people's sexual abilities. They found that most people can be sexually functional into their eighties.

Doing Away with the Double Standard. As a result of their studies, Masters and Johnson have come to believe that the double standard in sex, which has offered a set of permissive attitudes for men and another set of restrictive ones for women, must go. These double-standard attitudes have prevented many women from allowing themselves to enjoy their sexual feelings.

Masters and Johnson claim that we can have a rich and fulfilling sex life from maturation through old age. But in order to achieve this goal, a new process of sex education is required, which will do away with both ignorance and the double standard. Their therapy principles and techniques for overcoming sexual dysfunction will have a role in this process as professional people and the general public begin to understand and to apply them.

CHAPTER 2

What Are They Like?

Who are Masters and Johnson? What are they like? What sort of people venture into the study of human sexual response? Are Masters and Johnson odd, voyeuristic, sensationalistic—and perhaps especially perverse to want to observe human sexual functioning in a *laboratory*?

Masters describes himself as "old-fashioned and conservative," and he is. But traits that characterize him more accurately are persevering, determined, and questioning. Masters, fifty-four, is married and the father of a daughter and a son, both college students. He was an athlete in his youth and keeps in shape by jogging. He is of medium height and has gray hair, cut short, rimming his mostly bald head. He has a commanding face, with penetrating blue-green eyes his most dominant feature. Masters looks serious and business-like and extremely energetic, yet also kindly. Only after one gets to know him does his humor become apparent.

Masters' youth was spent in the Midwest. His father, Francis, was one of the first traveling district managers of the Pitney Bowes Company, the postage meter firm. His mother, Estabrooks Masters, still living in St. Louis, is a creative person who exudes great vitality. She ran the Masters household in lively fashion during all the years her husband traveled on his job, and her energies, talents, and imagination exerted considerable influence on her two sons. The family was Republican and church-going Episcopalian, and Masters has continued these affiliations.

Masters was born in Cleveland on December 27, 1915. He was a robust youngster with a lot of independent spirit. After two years of high school in Kansas City, he was sent East to Lawrenceville Preparatory School in New Jersey, and from there to Hamilton College in upper New York State. Masters' first love at college was English literature, but he took some premedical courses too. His plan was to teach English, but his younger brother, Frank, who had always wanted to be a doctor, persuaded him that he ought to give medical school a try. A brotherly rivalry existed between Bill and Frank, which prompted him to respond to the urging. He enrolled at the University of Rochester School of Medicine and Dentistry in the fall of 1938. Today, Masters' brother is a successful plastic surgeon who practices and teaches at the University of Kansas Medical School.

As a third-year medical student at Rochester, in 1942, Masters had already made up his mind to go into sex research. He had not thought out just how it would be done, but in a general way it was a field of study that interested him. After all, if a physiologist could learn all about respiration or some other basic body function, why couldn't someone study exactly how the sex organs work?

It is too simple to say that this complex man chose his life's work because it was an unknown area that needed to be explored. No doubt this was a part of it, but Masters is a private man, generally reserved in talking about his own motivations. Probably he was intrigued by the field of sex research more because it was forbidden than because it was unknown. "If someone says, 'You can't do that; it's never been done before,' it's just like holding a red flag up in front of me," says Masters. And he admits to having always been drawn to the untried, the unknown.

Masters was not exactly sure in those early days what specific training he would need. As a medical student at Rochester he had been inspired by the work of the distinguished reproductive biologist, Dr. George Corner, who was head of the department of Anatomy. After graduation from medical school in 1943, Masters came to St. Louis for his internship at Barnes Hospital, the teaching hospital for Washington University School of Medicine. Masters had been George Corner's last research assistant at Rochester. At it happened, the man for whom Masters went to work at Barnes—Willard Allen, head of Obstetrics and Gynecology—had been Corner's first research assistant.

Thus Masters followed the conventional avenues open to any bright, serious young physician who was interested in a research career. The men with whom he worked were distinguished, respected, and accomplished and had qualities he wished to emulate. Corner was famous for his work on ovarian hormones and the reproductive cycle, and Willard Allen had discovered the chemical formula for the female hormone, progesterone, when he was a third-year medical student at Rochester. "I came to St. Louis," Masters says, "because Willard Allen was the chairman of the department of Obstetrics and Gynecology. I also knew that in St. Louis I could work in endocrinology, and I thought this would be an important part of sexual function."

Endocrinology is important in sexology because the chemical secretions, known as endocrine hormones, which are transported through the bloodstream, regulate the responses of several organs including the sex organs. The female sex hormone, progesterone, for example, which is produced in the ovaries, prepares the uterus to receive a fertilized egg, thus enabling pregnancy to take place. The male sex hormone, testosterone, produced in the testicles, determines, among other things, secondary sex characteristics such as male body hair patterns and deepening of voice.

Masters had given some thought to becoming a psychiatrist, but decided against it because training in that field would not enable him to study his patients physically. As many sexologists did before him, Masters chose obstetrics and gynecology as his specialty. "I didn't know a damned thing about the female. I knew a few things about the male because I am one. I did think that I could learn something about the female from obstetrics and gynecology. If nothing else, I would know her anatomically. Did I think I was going to learn about sex in the female from obstetrics and gynecology? No, but at least a gynecologist performs surgery. He takes the female's reproductive system apart and puts it together again. That interested me. I always want to know how things work."

Masters took specialty training in three different areas of medicine that might relate to the little-known field of sex research. He studied pathology, internal medicine, and obstetrics and gynecology at Washington University. It was late June of 1947 when he finished his medical education at the age of thirty-two.

As a resident in obstetrics and gynecology in 1946, Masters had started his basic work in hormone replacement that led to his early recognition here and abroad. The radical approach of replenishing hormones in menopausal and postmenopausal women had never been tried before. Today, of course, it is accepted as a normal part of gynecologic practice. Between 1948 and 1959 Masters published more than forty scientific papers on the hormone problems of aging. He continued his basic research in hormones and aging for seven years after residency training before beginning his sexual-response research work at Washington University in July, 1954.

When Masters set up the Division of Reproductive Biology at Washington University, his first study subjects were mostly prostitutes. In those days no one believed that normal men and women would volunteer for the laboratory. One of the women in the preliminary study group had a Ph.D. in sociology and was supplementing her income by working as a call girl. As Masters relates it, "I had been talking with this girl for about an hour and a half listening to her attempt to tell me something about female sexual functioning, and it wasn't getting through at all. I didn't know what the woman was talking about. Finally, in utter frustration she said, 'Doctor, what you need is an interpreter because you are never going to know anything about women!' The more I thought about it the more I really knew how right she was. I was never going to know anything about female sexual expression because I could never experience it. At this stage of the game—this was in late 1955—I started to think that I should follow her advice. I began hunting for a female partner in 1956, and Gini joined me in January, 1957."

Masters was fortunate to have Virginia Johnson join

him as his research assistant. Divorced the previous year, Mrs. Johnson had registered with the Washington University placement bureau for a job and was interviewed and hired by Dr. Masters. He had set up demanding criteria for the person he needed; he was looking for an intelligent woman in her late twenties or early thirties who needed to work and who wanted to make a career of it. He also specified that she must have been married and divorced and have had at least one child. Masters works a very long work week, and he expected his assistant to work right along with him. If she were married, he reasoned, she would not be able to keep his hours.

Masters did not look for a female physician because the work involved a considerable professional gamble at that stage. He would have had to ask a young woman M.D. to put her degree on the line, so to speak, and he doubted that she would have been willing to do it. More important, Masters felt that professional training did not exempt a person from negative and judgmental attitudes in the mid-1950's.

Mrs. Johnson is a pretty, feminine woman, now in her mid-forties, who radiates an easy manner that makes patients relax quickly. She has always been deeply concerned with human relationships. Though professionally she is outgoing and empathetic, she is also, like Masters, an essentially private person. This is one of the reasons they have worked so well together over the years.

Mrs. Johnson was born Mary Virginia Eshelman on February 11, 1925, in Springfield, Missouri, in the Ozarks farm country. The only child, until her brother was born when she was twelve years of age, she describes her parents as highly intelligent and having a feeling for people that she believes was enhanced by living close to the land. "They both felt that a child of theirs could do no wrong," she comments. "With that kind of acceptance you never stopped trying. My parents could take good school grades and appropriate conduct for granted. Music, art, and making beautiful things were special, and for those talents, there was a special reverence." If a person played a musical instrument or sang, as Mrs. Johnson did, then, as she explains, "This was considered God-given. Everyone gathered to listen if you practiced."

Mrs. Johnson studied music at Drury College in Springfield and also attended business college. Then, a summer political job at the state capitol which lasted four years financed further musical studies before she enrolled at the University of Missouri.

At the university she became caught up in the availability of "so many things to be learned," especially in the fields of sociology and psychology, and eventually she abandoned her musical career to study human behavior. Oddly, she has never received a degree, although she has been a "professional student" throughout her adult life. In 1964 she registered as a Ph.D. candidate in psychology at Washington University, but then became so involved in the development of the Reproductive Biology Research Foundation that she was unable to complete the degree.

In 1950, she married George Johnson and had two children, a son and a daughter. Her husband was an engineering student who had an on-campus orchestra with which she sang. Her voice still plays a role in her present work; it conveys a feeling of warmth and sincerity immediately.

Masters and Johnson live quietly. Both keep informed in their world, but they do not have time for much of the rest of it. Their demanding work schedule, seven days a week, usually totaling eighty hours, does not allow for many close friendships outside their profession, nor for many outside activities. Neither has taken a vacation since 1954.

Masters enjoys an occasional night at a sports or musical event and the Sunday afternoon pro football games. He has much of the loner about him. Mrs. Johnson admits she would like to take in more concerts and cultural activities, and even go horseback riding occasionally, but there just does not seem to be enough time.

Asked why they work so hard, Masters says, "It's a compulsion. Basically we are driven by our lack of knowledge in an area that is incredibly important. When people seek our help they come as a marriage unit, and because they aren't functioning sexually they really don't have a marriage. We don't think that sex is the only thing in marriage, but it is usually a pretty poor marriage without it." Mrs. Johnson goes on with eloquence and conviction: "As far as we know, marriage is going to be around for a while. If in any way we can contribute to an ongoing interpersonal relationship that allows two people to live as fully as possible without handicap—this is what we want to do."

CHAPTER 3

How They Started

Many of Masters' medical colleagues in obstetrics and gynecology were initially vehemently opposed to his work in human sex research. As people first and doctors second, many physicians have the same restrictive attitudes about sex as the rest of the public.

Masters' inquisitiveness made apparent the essentially conservative attitudes of many obstetricians and gynecologists. Some years ago an elder statesman in obstetrics and gynecology walked up to him at a medical convention and said, "I want to tell you that you sicken me." This hostility was fairly representative of the profession, though few physicians voiced it quite so explicitly. Another time, an older colleague said to him, "Bill, I strongly disapprove of what you are doing. It certainly isn't obstetrics and gynecology. Furthermore, I must say that I've seen an awful lot more patients than you, and in all my life I have never had a patient in my office complain of a sexual disorder." Masters replied, "You know, I believe you."

Masters knew that such attitudes would make it impossible for him to study human sexual response unless he had an established reputation as a scientist and unless a university sponsored him at the start. His work on hormone replacement therapy satisfied the first requirement and Willard Allen helped him with the second. As head of the department of obstetrics and gynecology at Washington University, Dr. Allen was able to get permission from the dean of the medical school and the chancellor of the university for Masters to start his work in reproductive biology in 1953. Allen agreed that Masters should have a chance, meanwhile expressing his own reservations. But this was a crucial steppingstone; it permitted Masters to begin.

Masters was well aware that he would not have won any popularity contest with his colleagues in those days, but he also says that he had to let a lot of the opposition and furor go right over his head. He was so busy that the negative opinions of others did not really matter. "No one," Masters explained, "knew anything about sex in the mid-fifties, except Kinsey, who knew only what people were telling him. The fact that he did his studies was incredibly important. We wouldn't have been able to work if it hadn't been for Kinsey. Not for what he did, but because he did it." Masters sincerely believes that other investigators might have done the research better than he and Mrs. Johnson, but no one had university support. Indiana University was the first school to support human sex research in this country by backing Kinsey, and Washington University became the first medical school to do so when it supported Masters. Masters knew from the start that there were enormous risks in venturing into sex research, risks different from those in any other kind of research. "If you do cancer research for ten years and don't come up with anything noteworthy, nobody is going to question you professionally. I went into sex research with the full knowledge that I had to win. I had to come up with something or I would have been destroyed professionally. Even with results, sex research invites criticism."

Masters had been offered chairmanships of several departments of obstetrics and gynecology at medical schools before he began his sex research. After that the offers stopped. Older men in medicine who took irrevocable positions against Masters' work ten years ago have tended to stick to them. Many members of the disapproving group agreed that it was good to have answers to the physiologic questions about sex, but lamented that there was just no "nice" way of getting them. These doctors are beginning to retire now, and Masters says there is nowhere near their degree of resistance among physicians today.

In July, 1954, Washington University agreed to help finance a modest research program in reproductive biology for two years. Masters was given small quarters on the third floor of the St. Louis Maternity Hospital. After two years it was up to Masters to support himself, which he did with small grants from various individuals. Masters' first large grant came in 1957 from a businessman in St. Louis who gave his project $14,000. Fortunately, it was an unrestricted gift which Masters could use for paying study subjects. In 1958, Masters and Johnson received a $25,000-a-year grant from the National Institutes of Health, a branch of the United States Public Health Service. It was continued for four years and then was withdrawn. Masters says, "I don't quarrel with their cutting us off. I couldn't understand more. That many years ago, who was qualified to pass on our work? There really wasn't anybody." Various obstetricians, gynecologists, and psychiatrists who were judging on the merits of projects for the National Institutes of Health must have found it difficult. No one had ever done this work before, and it was dynamite in terms of potential controversy. The National Institutes of Health, or for that matter, any of the large foundations had never given money for anything that was as sociologically and culturally controversial as this.

Subsequently Masters approached the National Institutes of Health four times for grants and was refused each time. Masters confesses that the last time he applied and was rejected, in 1963, he spent more time writing the grant applications than he did in writing *Human Sexual Response* or *Human Sexual Inadequacy*. "I couldn't apply to NIH today if they invited me," he says. "I wouldn't have the three months necessary to write up the request. We honestly don't have the manpower at present to do this sort of thing. We just could not afford the time."

At the end of 1963 money difficulties forced Masters to move his research from its Washington University auspices and quarters. The university would not support a fully functioning reproductive biology division. Any donations for Masters' work had to be given through the university, and the university, as is customary, took a percentage for overhead. Since the grants were small, Masters' project received very little money. "We couldn't operate," he says impatiently. "We'd start something and have to stop; then we'd start again with a little money and stop. We were wasting time; we were grinding our gears."

In January of 1964, Masters rented space in a new building near the university and continued his work there supported by grants from individuals and his own gynecologic practice. Masters knew that this independent venture, the Reproductive Biology Research

Foundation, would negate an immediate chance of a professorship, an important consideration to a man who has spent his entire professional life in an academic environment. "The choice was mine," says Masters. "If I had stayed, I would have been too involved in university politics and administration. I simply couldn't be an administrator and do this type of research. It would have destroyed my chances to work, and wasted several years." If anything he is associated with is not progressing, Masters cannot be bothered with it. He felt that many professionals and the public were going to look askance at his work anyhow, whether he was with a university or on his own. Considering everything, it was best to leave. Masters confesses that he thrives on a certain amount of pressure, and going out alone provided a challenge he relished. He did, however, remain on the medical school staff as a part-time teacher, and last year was appointed to full professor.

The staff at the Reproductive Biology Research Foundation originally consisted of three people: Masters, Johnson, and one secretary. Now there are five therapists, with a sixth soon to join the Foundation, and a staff of twenty-five, including an office manager, Mrs. Wanda Bowen. Cotherapists Sallie Schumacher and Richard Spitz have been working with Masters and Johnson for a year. Dr. Schumacher is a clinical psychologist and mother of five, and Dr. Spitz is a pediatrician and a Lutheran minister. Raymond W. Waggoner, M.D., retired chairman of the department of Psychiatry at the University of Michigan School of Medicine and recent past president of the American Psychiatric Association, joined the group in July, 1970.

Masters had little or no money at the start and openly says that it has been a continual struggle to get enough financial backing to keep the Foundation going. There are still many research projects his staff cannot tackle because of lack of funds. As their work has become more accepted over the years, more grants and gifts have come their way, but essentially, Masters has had to go out and raise money for the Foundation. "I have strong feelings," Masters emphasizes, "about how people go about getting grants. If I had anything to do with research grants, I'd say, 'I'll give you the second fifty percent of the grant, but you have to come up with the first fifty percent.'"

Masters and Johnson have developed one of the best-equipped private chemical-biological laboratories in the country. All test equipment is automated, and its research and clinical potential is enormous. Under the direction of Dr. Gelson Toro, a biochemist, and his associate, Dr. Philip Ackermann, the laboratory conducts tests needed for research subjects and patients. In addition to other basic biologic research, new studies on testosterone hormone levels in the aging male are now beginning. The laboratory, known as the Missouri Clinical and Biochemical Laboratory, also does work for other physicians and research teams, and it is beginning to help the Foundation financially.

The interests of the Reproductive Biology Foundation range from basic research to care of patients. Its aims are to study the basic physiology of conception and its applications in the treatment of infertile couples; to conduct research in contraceptive physiology with clinical orientation to problems of population control; and to investigate the psychology of human sexual response and its applications in the treatment of human sexual inadequacy.

An administrative board of directors and a board of

consultive scientists directs Foundation activities. On the scientific advisory board are the well-known authorities Frank A. Beach, Ph.D., professor of psychology at the University of California at Berkeley; Lawrence Z. Freedman, M.D., of the department of Psychiatry at the University of Chicago; and John Rock, M.D., clinical professor emeritus of Gynecology at Harvard University. On the board of directors, in addition to Masters and Johnson, are Marion E. Bunch, Ph.D., chairman of the department of Psychology at Washington University; Frank Calderone, M.D., a noted public health official; Ethan A. Shepley, Jr., a St. Louis banker; Mrs. Richard B. Kallans, a leader in community activities in St. Louis; Emily H. Mudd, Ph.D., professor of Family Study in the department of Psychiatry, University of Pennsylvania Medical School; and Torrey N. Foster, a Cleveland, Ohio, attorney.

CHAPTER 4

Volunteers in the Laboratory: Who, How, and Why

As soon as it became known that Masters and Johnson were conducting laboratory research based on observing and studying human sexual functioning—the research which led to the publication of *Human Sexual Response*—there was curiosity about what sort of people would volunteer to take part in these studies. Initially Masters recruited prostitutes, because they were available for money and because they knew a lot about physical sex. The Ph.D. call girl who suggested that Masters get a female assistant was from this study group. After a year and a half of study, in which much useful information was gathered, Masters and Johnson decided that prostitutes were not suitable subjects for normal sexual response studies. Because they frequently experience sexual arousal without having orgasm, prostitutes often develop a chronic pelvic congestion which makes their physical reactions different from those of the average woman.

Subtly, Masters and Johnson let the word go out around the university that they were interested in studying normal volunteers. Since an academic community keeps informed and is usually more liberal than the rest of the populace, it did not take long for study subjects to show up. Many medical students and their wives participated, as did employees of the medical school and members of the community generally. Some were already patients of Masters. Everyone was assured at the start that identities would be kept absolutely secret.

Masters and Johnson were surprised at how easy it was to get people to volunteer. Study subjects were paid, so that was part of their motivation for participating, but many took part because they were interested in and concerned about their own body and its functioning. Some volunteers were obvious exhibitionists, and these were quickly eliminated as subjects. It was a little difficult to get older subjects to volunteer, but even this did not pose too great a problem. Study subjects were almost all whites, but a few blacks took part. Eventually Masters and Johnson selected 694 men and women from the 1,273 who applied. They ranged in age from eighteen to eighty-nine. Among them were 276 married couples; 106 women and thirty-six men were not married at the start of the research. Ninety-eight of the single people had been married previously.

All volunteers had to be capable of apparently normal sexual functioning; this was a prerequisite. They were given a thorough physical examination to determine if there were any abnormalities that might make such functioning impossible. Some were ruled out on this count. Also, if any volunteers showed signs of emotional instability, they were eliminated from the study. Volunteers were interviewed in depth by both Dr. Masters and Mrs. Johnson in order to obtain complete sexual and social histories, and all accepted test subjects were informed ahead of time about the exact nature of the research in which they were to participate. Orientation to the experiments themselves was explicit and complete. Each subject knew that he or she would be observed during coitus and that the various body responses would be recorded.

The laboratory room, in which all the studies took place, is plain with light green walls, moderate-sized, without windows. In it was a bed and scientific instruments that enabled Masters and Johnson to make recordings of blood pressure, heart rate, respiratory rate, brain-wave patterns, and other body activity during sexual excitement. They frequently had to design equipment themselves. Temperature and humidity of the laboratory were controllable, and the lighting adjustable.

Couples were asked to relax for a while in this laboratory bedroom, and then they were encouraged to engage in intercourse there, without being observed, before the recording of an actual experiment began. Once couples were relaxed and showed they could respond, they became a part of the study program. Those who could not, left the study. Couples were also told ahead of time that they would be observed during sexual activity not only by therapists but possibly by assistants, artists, and cameramen. Many experiments were filmed. The unmarried participants were involved mostly in research other than studies involving intercourse. Ejaculation by masturbation was studied in many single men, for example. Female responses were studied by the use of an artificial phallus which could be controlled voluntarily for size and for depth and rapidity of thrust. This equipment was made of plastic, and it was especially designed to allow observation through it. Masters and Johnson found that vaginal responses from the use of this device were exactly the same as the responses from coitus with a man. These responses of single men and women without partners were studied in detail and were important because they offered a comparison with couples' responses.

Men were not as reliable sexual performers as women. The anxiety produced by the necessity of having an erection made achieving erection difficult for a certain number of men. About 7,500 female sexual responses were studied, with only 118 failures to achieve orgasm when it was required. In approximately 2,500 male cycles studied, there were 220 failures.

Follow up with the volunteer subjects indicates that none suffered ill effects from participating in the laboratory experiments. In fact, many said the experience was beneficial.

Masters and Johnson have never insisted that their test subjects were average people. All they claim is that they were sexually responsive people. Studying sexually functional people made it possible to establish some of the physiologic facts of sexual response never observed and recorded before. Nor were Masters and Johnson's study subjects a cross-section of the population. Many were from the university community, a better-educated and more affluent group than the population in general.

The laboratory room where all of the findings for *Human Sexual Response* were recorded has now been emptied and the equipment disassembled. It is to be used for other purposes. All that one sees on looking into it at this writing is the special black baseboard with 220-volt outlets spaced every few inches around the entire room. These were originally needed as power sources for recording equipment. If funds become available, Masters hopes to build a new and better-equipped laboratory at the Foundation.

Masters and Johnson expected the general population to have its share of cranks, protesters, and late-Victorians who would object to human sex research, and for these individuals to express opposition. Although they have always been alert to public opinion, they went right on with their work, ignoring whatever abuse came their way from such persons.

The first major attack from the intellectual community, an attack which had to be taken seriously, came in November, 1964, when Leslie H. Farber, a psychoanalyst, blasted Masters and Johnson's research in an article titled, "I'm Sorry Dear," in *Commentary* magazine. In the article Dr. Farber deplored what he called the "mechanization" in Masters and Johnson's approach to sex. He claimed that they were dehumanizing the experience and that there was too much emphasis in their work on female orgasm. It was a wittily done piece and commanded wide attention.

What Dr. Farber failed to understand was that Masters and Johnson were not depersonalizing sex—far from it; what they were trying to do was find out what really happened during sexual excitement so that physicians and other therapists could help people who cannot respond. Masters and Johnson deplore the depersonalization of sex by our culture. They deplore the false values and the double standards that have caused so many people to regard their sexuality as unnatural and unacceptable. By observing people in the laboratory, Masters and Johnson were not equating lovemaking with research. They believe lovemaking will be more natural and fulfilling and brought into perspective as a real part of our lives, if ignorance about it is replaced with knowledge. The well-known psychiatrist and sex educator, Dr.

Harold I. Lief, writing in the SIECUS newsletter, said about the Farber attack:

> "If sex has become a commodity dispassionately bought and sold instead of a basic aspect of human feeling and interaction, the blame must be fixed on our culture and its institutions rather than on sober, scientific investigators of a vital but hitherto neglected area of human research. Before man can determine what is *right,* he must find out what *is!*"

Before the Farber attack, Masters and Johnson spoke only at scientific meetings from which the press was barred. Whenever they spoke there was always a stir around the meeting hall because of the seemingly sensational aspects of their films or talks. Doctors are fairly jaded about most aspects of body functioning, but news of a Masters' presentation at a medical convention always created great interest. Their material was bound to be original; no one had shown films at a scientific meeting of couples having intercourse, or illustrations that showed, for example, what the inside of the vagina looked like when a woman was sexually stimulated. Yet Masters and Johnson felt their work was vulnerable to attack during the experimental stages before statistically significant data were available. Therefore, they avoided press publicity, hoping they would not have to defend their research until they were ready.

Now, however, after the Farber article, they became concerned that an avalanche of unfavorable publicity might bury their work. They feared for its future if it were not presented accurately and fairly, and so they decided to go ahead with the preparation of *Human*

Sexual Response somewhat earlier than had originally been intended.

Masters and Johnson had been publishing articles about their work in the *Western Journal of Surgery, Obstetrics and Gynecology,* a respected but small specialty journal. Most of the nationally circulated journals had refused to take their papers for publication. As a result, many of Masters and Johnson's major findings had never appeared before the publication of *Human Sexual Response.* This is partly why the book created so much interest among professionals.

Masters knew exactly what he wanted in a publisher. He realized that his book could be played up in a sensational way, and that was what he did not want. He wanted to work with a medical publisher so that the book would be bought by physicians and other professionals who need information about sexual functioning. Furthermore, he wanted a medical publisher who appreciated and understood his material and would reproduce it with dignity. Thus he chose the medical division of the 133-year-old Boston firm of Little, Brown and Company.

Masters insisted that *Human Sexual Response* was to be advertised to professionals only through traditional medical publishing outlets, and that it was to be treated exactly as the publisher would treat any other of its medical publications. If the general public wanted to buy it, they could, of course, and they did; but neither Masters and Johnson nor Little, Brown thought that public demand would be large, since *Human Sexual Response* was highly technical and not easy for the non-medically trained person to understand. They were wrong. Masters was hailed as a new Kinsey, and *Human Sexual Response* became a best seller.

CHAPTER 5

Human Sexual Response: The First Masters and Johnson Report

If problems of sexual functioning are to be treated successfully, the first question that must be answered is how the sex organs work—what happens to the body when a man or a woman responds to effective stimulation. Masters has said many times that to accomplish anything in medicine one must go to the laboratory first, and this is exactly what he did. In *Human Sexual Response*, Masters and Johnson reported their observations of the sexual responses of men and women in the laboratory during an eleven-year study. This chapter describes the most important of their findings.

The Sexual Response Cycle

That first study showed similarities between the sexes never before appreciated. One of the most unexpected was that the basic sexual response cycle is the same for both men and women. The cycle has four phases: the excitement phase, the plateau phase, the orgasmic phase, and the resolution phase.

The *excitement phase* is initiated by whatever is sexually stimulating for a particular individual. If stimulation is strong enough, excitement builds quickly, but if it is interrupted or if it becomes objectionable, this phase becomes extended or the cycle may be stopped. If effective sexual stimulation is continued, it produces increased levels of sexual tension that lead ultimately to orgasm. This increased tension is called the *plateau phase*. If the individual's drive for sexual release in this phase is not strong enough, or if stimulation ceases to be effective or is withdrawn, a man or woman will not experience orgasm, but will enter a prolonged period of gradually decreasing sexual tensions. The climactic or *orgasmic phase,* a totally involuntary response, consists of those few seconds when the body changes resulting from stimulation reach their maximum intensity. During the *resolution phase,* after orgasm, there is a lessening of sexual tensions as the person returns to the unstimulated state. Women are capable of having another orgasm if there is effective stimulation during this phase. The resolution period in the male includes a time, which varies among individuals, when restimulation is impossible. This is called the *refractory period.*

In both sexes, the basic responses of the body to sexual stimulation are myotonia (increased muscle tension) and vasocongestion (filling of the blood vessels with fluid), especially in the genital organs, causing swelling. Of course these basic physiologic responses take on a different appearance in a man than they do in a woman. Interestingly enough, the basic physiologic sexual responses remain the same regardless of the kind of stimulation—coital, manipulative, mechanical, or fantasy. However, intensity and duration of the responses vary with the method of stimulation used.

Masturbation produced the most intense experiences observed in the laboratory, partner manipulation the next, and intercourse the least.

Female Response

The Excitement Phase. Within ten to thirty seconds after the beginning of any effective sexual stimulation, a woman responds with the production of vaginal lubrication. The source of this lubrication was thought to be the cervix (opening of the uterus into the vagina) or some small glands called Bartholin's glands in the labia minora (inner lips of the vagina) (Fig. 1). Actually, neither of these is the source. Masters and Johnson suggested from their observations that filling of the blood vessels and subsequent swelling around the vagina causes some of the fluid in the tissues to pass through the membranous vaginal wall. Women who have had their reproductive organs removed respond to sexual stimulation with vaginal lubrication, and so do women who were born without sex organs and have surgically constructed artificial vaginas. This is reasonable evidence that the cervix is not a source of vaginal lubrication. Bartholin's glands have been observed to secrete a small amount of fluid, but not nearly enough to lubricate the vagina.

In addition to lubricating, the inner two thirds of the vagina lengthens and distends, preparing to accept the penis. As sexual tensions progress to plateau level (the period between excitement and orgasm), the uterus elevates, pulling on the vagina and making it much wider. The vaginal walls, purplish red in an unstimulated

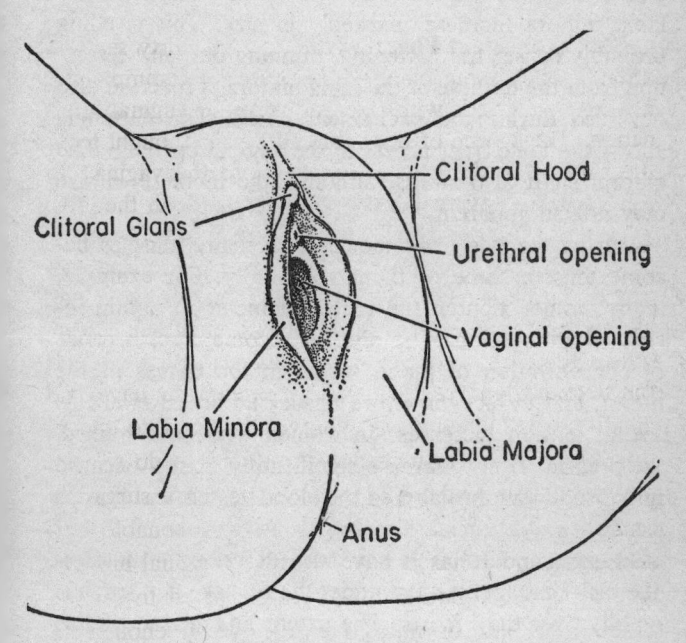

Figure 1. The external genitals of the human female.

state, change slowly to a darker hue because of engorgement with blood.

Engorgement of tissues, the cause of the vaginal color changes, also causes alterations in the female external sex organs during the excitement phase. The blood vessels in the labia minora (Fig. 1), become filled, and the labia minora increase markedly in size. This swelling probably causes the flattening, thinning out, and retraction from the midline of the labia majora, a reaction also observed during the excitement phase. The flattening allows the male freer access to the vaginal opening. The clitoral shaft also swells, although the increase in size may not be apparent.

During the late excitement phase many muscles become tensed, some of them voluntarily. For example, many women tighten the rectal sphincter to obtain increased stimulation. The nipples become erect because of concentration of blood serum in the tissues of the breast, and in fact the entire unsuckled breast swells as sexual tension increases. In women who have nursed, the breasts do not increase significantly in size because milk production has altered the blood vessels and fibrous tissues.

Masters and Johnson have also described a measles-like rash that appears just under the rib cage and spreads rapidly over the breasts. The extent and spread of this "sex flush" was first noted when lights for the filming of sexual activity in the laboratory increased both the illumination and the skin temperature of the subjects, thus defining the rash more clearly. Seventy-five percent of the female study subjects developed this rash.

The Plateau Phase. The outer third of the vagina becomes slightly enlarged during the excitement phase. In the plateau phase, the second phase of the response cycle, this area becomes so engorged with venous blood that the vaginal opening decreases by at least a third. Masters and Johnson have called this distended part of the vaginal wall the "orgasmic platform" (Fig. 2).

The engorged labia minora undergo a vivid color change in this phase which is one of the most striking physiologic alterations to develop during the female response cycle. In women who have never given birth, these structures change from pink to bright red; and in women who have had children, from red to a deep wine color. No woman has ever been observed to have orgasm who did not experience this color change, which is called the "sex skin reaction" (Fig. 2).

During the plateau phase, the clitoris retracts from its unstimulated position to a relatively inaccessible place under the clitoral hood (Fig. 1). This is a universal and extremely significant response. Effective coital technique related to it is discussed further on in this chapter.

The tissues around the nipples fill with fluid, making it seem that nipple erection has been partly lost. The sex flush spreads to all areas of the breasts, chest, and abdomen and sometimes to other body surfaces as well. It reaches its peak in color as well as extent of distribution in the plateau phase and then disappears rapidly with orgasm.

The Orgasmic Phase. At the moment of orgasm, breathing is at least three times as fast as the normal rate; heart rate is more than double, and blood pressure increases by a third. Most of the body muscles tense. Precisely what triggers the orgasmic response is not known, but it begins with contractions starting in the orgasmic platform in the outer third of the vagina. This platform contracts rhythmically as sexual tension is released. The contractions begin at 0.8-second intervals,

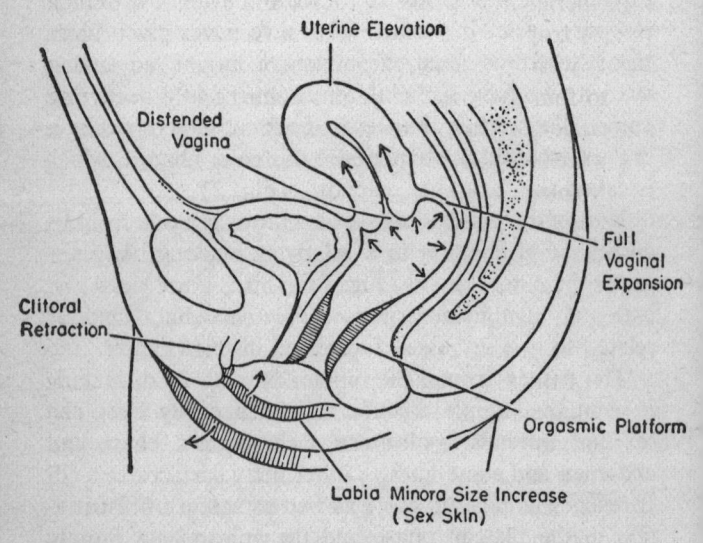

Figure 2. Female internal genitals, plateau phase of the sexual response cycle.

and recur from three to fifteen times, decreasing in frequency and intensity after the first few. Uterine contractions may begin at almost the same time as the vaginal contractions, but these usually do not occur in a definite pattern. Sometimes the external rectal sphincter contracts too. There is variation in the intensity of the experience among individuals and even in the same woman from one time to the next. Occasionally orgasm begins with a spastic contraction of the vagina lasting two to four seconds before proceeding to the recurring contractions. This spastic contraction may parallel a man's feeling of inevitability just before ejaculation.

Physiologically, orgasm is a release of the muscular spasm and engorgement of blood vessels built up by sexual stimulation. Subjectively, it is the experience of peak physical pleasure. For women the attainment of this peak is based on a variety of psychologic and social factors of prime importance but which are outside the scope of the first Masters and Johnson book. In American culture men are more body-oriented, while women respond to the total person and the total situation. Whether this is entirely a cultural phenomenon or whether it has a biologic basis is not known. The psychologic and social influences in a woman's sex life are discussed more fully in Chapter 13, Orgasmic Dysfunction in Women.

The Resolution Phase. The sex flush and the swelling around the nipples disappear rapidly after orgasm, and frequently a film of perspiration covers much of the body at the same time. The clitoris, which has been retracted and is invisible during the plateau and orgasmic phases, returns to its normal position five to ten seconds after orgasmic contractions stop. If there has been an observable swelling of the clitoris during the excitement phase, this gradually disappears five to ten minutes after orgasm.

The congestion in the outer third of the vagina, "the orgasmic platform," disappears quickly, making the opening of the vagina wider. The labia majora also return rapidly to their unstimulated size after orgasm has taken place. As the cervix descends to its unstimulated position, the inner two thirds of the vagina becomes less distended and returns to its usual size in three or four minutes.

After orgasm, the strained features of the woman relax, and the clutching and other spastic muscular reactions dissipate. Some women, most frequently those who have not had children, have the urge to urinate. This is because pelvic structures that have not been stretched by giving birth hold the penis in a position which irritates the urinary bladder.

Male Response

The Excitement Phase. A man's first physiologic response to sexual stimulation is erection of the penis. Erection is caused by engorgement with blood and is the parallel response to lubrication of the vagina in women. A full erection may result from a small amount of excitement and may be maintained for a long time by careful control of stimulation. During an intentionally prolonged excitement phase, with variation of stimuli, the penis may get soft and then hard again several times. Any distraction, such as a loud noise or a change in the environment, may cause a partial or complete loss of erection in spite of stimulation.

With increasing excitement, the skin of the scrotum becomes tense, congested and thick, decreasing the space within the scrotal sac. The testes rise higher in the scrotum. If there is a long period of sex play, the scrotum may relax again and the testes descend, even though the penis is still erect. However, when sexual tensions progress to the plateau phase, the scrotal wall thickens, and the testes elevate again quickly.

Frequently sexual excitement causes nipple erection and swelling in men. Direct manipulation of the male breast is not a usual part of heterosexual foreplay, say Masters and Johnson, although it is common among male homosexuals.

In men, and in women as well, there is a total body response to increasing sexual excitement. Gentle petting and caressing proceed to more restless, rapid, and forceful movement. There is also increasing spasm in the long muscles of the legs and arms, increased tension in the muscles of the abdomen, and more rapid breathing.

The Plateau Phase. In the second stage of sexual response, the same measles-like rash develops in the male as in the female, but it is a less frequent occurrence in men. It begins just under the rib cage and spreads over the chest, neck, and face. It is evidence of intense sexual tensions, and Masters and Johnson observed that it does not develop even in susceptible men during every response cycle.

In both sexes, but perhaps more pronounced in the male, the most apparent bodily response in the plateau phase is increased muscular tension. There is involuntary spasm of the muscles of the face, neck, and abdomen in both men and women. Spasm in the long muscles of the limbs depends upon the position of the partners. During masturbation there is a voluntary increase in the rate of hand movement and an involuntary increase in pressure applied to the genitals.

The muscles of the buttocks and thighs, which are most actively involved in pelvic thrusting, are at first voluntarily controlled in both sexes, but their motion progresses to a rapid forceful thrusting that is essentially an involuntary reaction. This is especially true of the male who rarely withdraws his penis more than halfway from the vagina as he approaches orgasm.

At the beginning of intercourse, the legs of a woman lying on her back are spread apart, but as tension increases, she brings them closer together, finally straining involuntarily against the man's thighs. The leg and arm muscles of a man in the superior position are contracted voluntarily at first to support his weight, but during the moments of intense sexual tension just before orgasm, these muscles contract in an essentially involuntary manner. A man who is masturbating while lying on his back has the same tendency to bring his legs tightly together as does a woman who is lying on her back during intercourse.

Although the penis has been fully erect since the first seconds of the excitement phase, the area around the ridge at the penile glans (head of the penis) increases in diameter as orgasm approaches. Sometimes, the glans deepens in color just before ejaculation, but this is not as marked as the sex skin color change in women.

But the end of the plateau phase, elevation of the testes is fully accomplished. This is an important reaction, because if the testes do not elevate, as happens sometimes in older men, the pressure of the ejaculation is greatly reduced. Full elevation of the testes indicates that orgasm is imminent. Masters and Johnson were the first to describe an increase in testicular size from fifty to one hundred percent during the plateau phase. This is another example of vasocongestion (filling of the tissues with fluid) as a response to sexual stimulation.

An additional reaction occurring in the plateau phase is the emission of a few drops of seminal fluid from the penis before the true ejaculate. This is likely to occur when the male has been sexually excited for a relatively long time and has delayed his orgasm.

The Orgasmic Phase. As ejaculation becomes imminent, breathing becomes much faster, and heart rate and blood pressure rise just as they do in women. There is increasing muscular tension all over the body.

Orgasm in males occurs in two stages, the first beginning immediately prior to ejaculation, when men experience a feeling of inevitability, after which they cannot hold back from the climax. This feeling is caused by contractions of the testes, prostate gland, and seminal vesicles as they collect the sperm and seminal fluid and expel them into the entrance of the urethra (the canal leading from the urinary bladder to the outside of the penis) (Fig. 3).

During the second stage of orgasm, the actual ejaculation of the seminal fluid through the urethral canal and out of the penis is caused by contractions of the urethra and muscles of the penis. In young men this pressure is great enough to expel the ejaculate a few feet from the penis if it is outside the vagina. The sensation of contractions is joined by a sensation of the presence of the seminal fluid. The prostate and penile contractions begin at 0.8-second intervals, just as they do in the female orgasmic platform, and decrease in intensity and frequency after the first few. The rectal sphincter also may contract involuntarily with the first two to four urethral contractions.

A large ejaculate is subjectively more pleasurable than

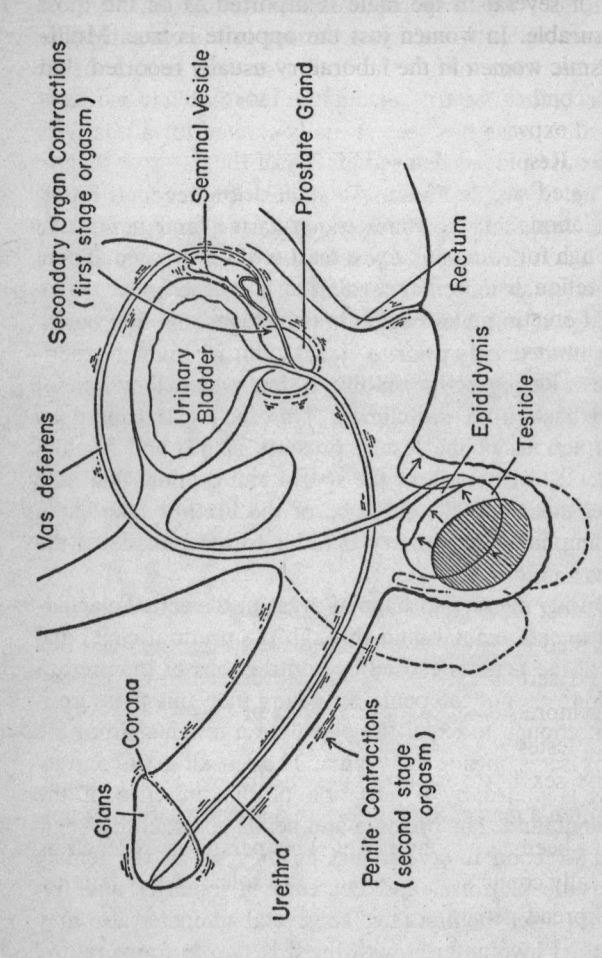

Figure 3. Male genitals, orgasmic phase of the sexual response cycle.

a small amount, which may account for the fact that the first of several in the male is reported to be the most pleasurable. In women just the opposite is true. Multiorgasmic women in the laboratory usually reported that the second or third orgasm is the most intense and prolonged experience.

The Resolution Phase. Return of the penis to its unstimulated size occurs in two well-defined stages. After ejaculation, half the erection usually is lost very quickly, although for some unknown reason this may not happen if erection had been present for a long time. Further loss of erection, the second stage of the resolution phase, is a slower process which may be retarded even more by keeping the penis in the vagina or by holding the partner close. It may be speeded by standing up or other distractions. The glans is very sensitive in some men right after ejaculation. If continued containment, thrusting, or stroking after ejaculation is painful, Masters and Johnson emphasize that a man should communicate this to his partner.

In most men the scrotal wall quickly reverts to its uncongested state, and the testes descend rapidly into the relaxed scrotal sac. In others the decongestion occurs much more slowly, lasting an hour or two with lowering of the testes also delayed.

The sex flush disappears immediately after orgasm, and often a man will break out in a sweat whether or not he has been active physically. This perspiratory reaction is usually confined to the palms and soles, but sometimes widespread perspiration occurs.

The Significance of the First Masters and Johnson Report

Masters and Johnson dared to observe and to measure sexual responses in the same way that physiologists have studied the lungs, the digestive system, and other body functions. Considering the strong taboos still operating against such investigations, the fact that the studies were made at all signifies a gradual acceptance of sex research. Although Masters and Johnson were criticized after publication of *Human Sexual Response* for their supposedly mechanistic view of sex, they themselves have always stressed the significance of their laboratory findings in relation to the treatment of sexual problems. Long before the results of their laboratory work were reported, their treatment program for sexually inadequate couples had begun. From their basic physiologic studies, they were able to present in their first report about human sexual and reproductive function which have practical relevance to everyone's sex life. They also exploded, once and for all, some prevalent and extremely harmful fallacies. These facts and fallacies are discussed in the following sections.

Role of the Clitoris in Sexual Stimulation. Misinformation about the response of the clitoris during sexual excitement and intercourse abounds. The clitoris is both the receiver and transmitter of female sexual feelings. As a receiver organ, its nerve endings and blood vessels respond to sexual stimulation, and as a transmitter organ it produces the subjective feeling of sexual arousal in a woman. This feeling has been described as a "deep pelvic fullness and warmth (possibly vasoconcentration)

... a feeling of local irritation, expansive urge, need for release ..."[1]

Earlier investigators tried to correlate the intensity of a woman's arousal with the size, anatomic position, or amount of swelling of the clitoris. The idea that size could be of importance is obviously related to the false idea, to be discussed later, that the size of the penis is related to virility. An anatomic position of the clitoris which would supposedly allow better contact with the penis during intercourse was also said to heighten female responsiveness, and the same was claimed for obvious swelling of the clitoris. Masters and Johnson have observed in the laboratory that none of these variables is related to responsiveness or orgasmic ability in women.

Because the clitoris retracts under its hood during heightened sexual excitement (Fig. 1), it becomes relatively inaccessible either to stimulation by hand or to the thrusting penis. Unfortunately, the writers of marriage manuals, recognizing the clitoris as the organ of female sexuality, instruct the male to stimulate it manually and to keep the penis in contact with it during intercourse. The result of following these instructions is that the inexperienced man loses the clitoris as it retracts during the plateau phase and frustrates the woman with his "textbook" attempts to find it. If he tries to stimulate it with his penis while thrusting in the male superior position, he will have to move in a direction that is painful for a woman whose vagina has not been stretched somewhat by childbearing. Besides, the man will not be able to penetrate deeply, and the partners will lose the pleasure of that maneuver. Actually, the clitoris is stimulated during intercourse without any special effort because every

---

[1] *HSR*, p. 62.

thrust causes traction on the clitoral hood, which puts pressure on the clitoris itself.

Although marriage manuals stress clitoral foreplay, very little has been said about how to do it and how much to do it. By watching women masturbate in the laboratory, Masters and Johnson noted a variety of clitoral manipulative techniques. Actually, no two women among their subjects masturbated the same way. Most often they stimulated the entire genital area, which causes a clitoral response regardless of whether that organ is directly touched. The result of overall manipulation is a slower arousal, but it leads to a fully satisfying climax, and it is less likely to be painful or irritating. These laboratory observations were enormously helpful in treating women unable to have orgasm (Chapter 13).

Manipulation of the clitoris may be painful, especially when it is done too hard or too long. Very few masturbating women manipulate the clitoral glans (head of the clitoris), and those who do usually restrict it to the excitement phase. Most often they stimulate one side of the clitoral shaft. Since women use such a large variety of automanipulative techniques, a man will satisfy his partner best by asking her what she likes and by encouraging communication.

Women usually continue masturbating actively during orgasm, just as they demand continued thrusting in the climactic phase of intercourse. In contrast, most men will penetrate deeply and maintain that position without moving during ejaculation. Some women can have several orgasms during a single episode of automanipulation when they are free to please themselves only, without the distractions of a partner.

Clitoral and Vaginal Orgasms—Separate or the Same? Masters and Johnson have proved false the notion of separate vaginal and clitoral orgasms. An orgasm is an orgasm; there are not two different kinds. Ever since Freud advanced the idea that there were two kinds of orgasms, the vaginal being the one psychologically mature women were supposed to have, this has been a point of controvrsy. Many writers, mostly men, have supported Freud's view. Direct observation of clitoral and vaginal responses shows that the orgasmic contractions take place in the vagina and the uterus no matter what erotic areas are stimulated or what technique is used.

Simultaneous Orgasms. Another canard of the marriage manuals relating to orgasm is that the couple's attainment of simultaneous climaxes is a mark of superior sexual achievement. *This simply is not true. Making the effort to coordinate such basically involuntary responses starts the partners observing themselves mentally, rather than losing themselves in the feelings of lovemaking.* As Masters and Johnson point out in *Human Sexual Inadequacy*, observing oneself during intercourse, which they call "assuming a spectator role," can lead to impotence in the male and inability to have orgasm in the female.

Role of the Vagina in Reproduction. Many investigators have considered the possibility that the environment within the vagina has a role in reproduction. They have done studies using semen obtained by masturbation and placed in an artificial acid environment like that of the normal vagina. Although these studies were useful, they could not measure the effects of other substances present in the normally functioning vagina, such as hormones, infectious agents, and the lubricating material which appears on the vaginal walls during excitement. By examining specimens of semen immediately after ejaculation into the vagina, Masters and Johnson demonstrated that some women produce a substance that kills sperm cells within minutes of ejaculation. The contraceptive possibilities of this substance have yet to be explored because the Foundation does not have the funds for the basic research. In most women, the lubricating material exerts a positive effect on fertility by reducing vaginal acidity, but here again, more studies are needed to define explicitly the effect of vaginal environment on reproduction.

The Artificial Vagina. The sexual responses of seven women born without vaginas were studied by Masters and Johnson and reported in their first book. All these women had had vaginas surgically constructed from their other pelvic tissues. The same sexual response cycle occurred in these women as in other laboratory subjects except that lubrication of the vaginal walls took place in thirty to forty seconds after stimulation rather than in ten to thirty seconds. Orgasm also occurred in the same way as it did in normal women, with the formation of an orgasmic platform which contracts at climax. The psychosexual and social problems of these women were not discussed in the first book, but there is no doubt that surgical treatment makes it physically possible for them to live normal sex lives.

Sexual Response During Menstruation. That sexual intercourse during menstruation will be painful or harmful for the woman is a prevalent myth, and many cultures regard as taboo any sexual activity during that time. Actually, there is no physiologic reason for continence during the menstrual flow. The question is rather one of individual preference: if one partner finds sexual activity disagreeable during menstruation, the other partner should forbear. Masters and Johnson reported that only thirty-three of 331 women questioned objected to sexual activity during their menstrual flow. The rest either had no objection or said they wanted sex especially during the latter half of the period. Forty-three women said that they masturbated at the beginning of their periods because orgasm relieved their cramps.

Sexual Response During Pregnancy. Masters and Johnson learned that *physically* much of the response cycle is unchanged during pregnancy. Three major differences were noted in the responses of six pregnant women studied anatomically and physiologically. First, a much greater amount of congestion was constantly present in all the pelvic organs. Second, there was a noticeable increase in vaginal lubrication during the excitement phase, probably related to the congestion. Third, the last phase of the response cycle, the resolution phase, was drastically different from that in the nonpregnant state because orgasm during pregnancy did not completely relieve congestion in the sex organs. After delivery, a woman's physiologic responses to sexual stimulation were greatly reduced, returning to normal only after three months. But Masters and Johnson found that this lessened physiologic response did not always correspond with sexual desire.

A hundred and one women and seventy-nine of their husbands were interviewed during a pregnancy and shortly after delivery about their sexual responses from a *subjective* point of view. The questions were focused around sexual interest, activities, and attitudes.

Sleepiness, chronic fatigue, nausea, and fear of causing miscarriage were reported to affect sex interest and response adversely during the first three months in most women who had no previous children. Most women who had children said their sex lives remained about the same.

In the second three months, eighty percent of the women, regardless of whether or not they had been pregnant before, reported that they were sexually much more responsive than before pregnancy. They dreamed more about sex and fantasied more, and in fact planned more for sexual activities. Because the enlarging uterus compresses the veins in the pelvic area, excitement phase vasocongestion is constantly present in pregnant women. Masters and Johnson say that there probably is a direct relation between this chronic pelvic congestion and the increased sexuality reported subjectively by women in the second trimester.

Most women reported a gradually decreasing interest in sex during the last three months. However, three quarters of the study subjects had been told by their doctors not to have intercourse from a month to three months before delivery, and this undoubtedly conditioned their attitudes. In addition, the increasing physical exertion necessary to care for other children and to do the housework made them more tired than usual. However, when they did have intercourse they surprised themselves with their responsiveness and orgasmic ability.

The women were interviewed for the last time during the third month after delivery. About half the group described their sexual tensions to be lower than usual. The other half had varying amounts of sexual interest, but nursing mothers had the most. All the nursing mothers were sexually stimulated by suckling. Three women said they had orgasm while nursing, and plateau phase tension was reported frequently. A few women felt very guilty about their sexual response to suckling. Although this phenomenon was reported before Masters and Johnson's study, and happens to most nursing women, none of the literature about the advantages of breast feeding mentions this interesting dividend.

Thirty-one of the seventy-nine husbands interviewed said they withdrew gradually from sex with their wives during the last three months of pregnancy. Some men really not not know why they did this, and some reported fears of hurting their wives or babies. Half of the women in the group were concerned about the long period of continence before and after delivery, and they provided noncoital sexual relief for their husbands during this time. Eighteen men in the study group reported extramarital activity during the continence period. Some men said they understood and respected the prohibition of intercourse; others said they did not. But none of these men, though many were college graduates, had any information about how their wives might feel or respond after delivery.

There are some legitimate reasons to be concerned with sexual activity during pregnancy. Occasionally during the third trimester, the uterus contracts spastically with orgasm, and the baby's heart rate slows, but this reaction dissipates quickly, leaving no evidence of effects on the baby. However, since orgasm causes the uterus to contract, women who have had many miscarriages are often advised to avoid intercourse during the first trimester. Masters and Johnson have shown that the uterine contractions caused by masturbating to orgasm are more intense than those caused by intercourse. Women susceptible to spontaneous abortion should thus be cautioned about all erotic activity.

Labor has been reported following intercourse or masturbation near the delivery date; however, nothing abnormal happened to the baby or mother. Whether sexual activity can start premature labor is not known, and of course, this is an important question. The position of the baby in relation to the birth canal late in pregnancy would possibly make a difference. Masters and Johnson feel that a lot of unhappiness could be avoided if physicians would evaluate patients individually and base their advice about sexual activity on the situation of each husband and wife. At the very least, advice should be given about ways to provide relief for the husband and about positions for intercourse during pregnancy. Many people think that any sexual activity except heterosexual intercourse in the all-American (man-on-top) position is perverted. They should be told that this is not true.

Phallic Truths and Fallacies. The role of the penis in urination and reproduction is clearly established, well understood, and furthermore easily accepted by most people. But its role as the primary receiver of sexual stimuli in men and a transmitter of sexual stimuli for both sexes is surrounded with misunderstandings. No doubt these misunderstandings and the reluctance to study the penis as a sensate organ have been detrimental to sexual well-being.

Probably one of the most common phallic fallacies is that the size of a man's penis is directly related to his virility and to the pleasure he can give a woman during intercourse. Although acceptance of this fallacy as fact gives a psychologic boost to the owners of large members (and possibly to their mates as well), there is no scientific basis for this belief.

In fact, penile size is less variable than people think. The soft penis does vary in size from individual to individual, but this variation is much less during erection.

Masters and Johnson observed smaller penises to double in size at the height of sexual excitement, while larger penises generally did not increase that much proportionally. Eighty men's sex organs were measured three times while soft and three times while hard. One of the measurements was taken during masturbation, and two were taken immediately on withdrawal just before ejaculation. There is no evidence to support the idea that a larger penis gets significantly bigger with full erection than does a smaller penis.

Even if there were significant differences in size among erect organs, one would have to consider what happens to the vagina during intercourse. The vagina is a potential, not an actual space, and as described previously, it expands somewhat with sexual excitement involuntarily. During entry, the distensible vaginal walls expand further just enough to accommodate the penis.

Another mistaken idea about penile size is that taller, heavier men have bigger penises than small men. Masters and Johnson's study showed that there is no relation between a man's body size and the size of his penis. A study subject who was five feet eleven inches tall and weighed 178 pounds had the smallest penis, measuring just under two and a half inches, and the subject with the largest penis, five and a half inches in the flaccid state, was five feet seven inches tall and weighed 152 pounds.

Almost all men in the study group believed that circumcision made the glans (head of the penis) more sensitive to sexual stimulation. They thought, therefore, that circumcised men had more difficulty achieving ejaculatory control. Masters and Johnson showed that there was no difference in the responses of circumcised and uncircumcised men to stimulation of the glans.

The most bizarre phallic fallacies are related to masturbation. Why these are so forceful and so ubiquitous is difficult to understand since masturbation is virtually a universal human activity. All the members of the study group said they masturbated, usually beginning right after puberty. Even though almost everybody does it, dire consequences from acne to insanity have been erroneously predicted, especially for boys. Boys especially are likely to be the victims of an admonishing mother's dire warning, "It will fall off if you keep doing that!"

Men have individual techniques of masturbating, just as women do, even though more boys watch each other in this activity than do girls. Most men stroke the shaft of the penis, although some do it harder and faster and use a stronger grip than others. Some men like to stimulate the glans only, either by rubbing it or pulling at it. They increase the rate of stroking with increasing sexual tension, until ejaculation begins. Then, most men stop stroking or do it much more slowly. Many men hold the penis tightly during orgasm. This kind of response is usually observed during intercourse also; the man penetrates as deeply as possible and stops thrusting. Some men do continue stroking during ejaculation, and these same men usually continue thrusting during orgasm in intercourse.

A frequently expressed fear of men under forty in the study population was that excessive masturbation would take away a man's strength or cause mental illness. Yet no one could name a person who had been so afflicted, and no one could really say for sure how much he thought was too much. A man who masturbated once a month thought that maybe once a week would be excessive, and a man who did it two or three times a day questioned whether five or six times a day wouldn't lead to a "case of nerves." No one in the group thought he himself was masturbating too much. The idea that masturbation is physically debilitating, immoral, or at least demeaning is firmly entrenched in American culture. But there simply is no evidence that it causes anything more or less than relief of sexual tensions.

Another common phallic fallacy, perhaps the most widely accepted of all, is that men necessarily become impotent as they get older. Masters and Johnson have shown that this idea is absolutely false. Some of their most startling findings have to do with aging men and women. How sexual responses in the aging differ from those of younger people and how the Foundation approaches the sexual problems of the aging are discussed in Chapter 16, "Sex in the Aging."

Masters and Johnson's work in the laboratory is the basis for most of their current treatment program. Their research disproves many old wives' tales which are barriers to sexual fulfillment. Even more important, as Masters puts it, "No one really knew what sexual function was. We went to the laboratory first. Now we know what we are trying to accomplish when we treat people who are dysfunctional."

CHAPTER 6

After Publication of Human Sexual Response

Rumors about *Human Sexual Response* multiplied as publication approached, although Little, Brown had made no effort to tell even professionals about it. Newspaper reporters, magazine editors, television and radio commentators, and other publishers called for information. They wanted to know just what was going on in so-called conservative Boston. Magazines wanted to buy serialization rights, to which Little, Brown said no. Paperback publishers wanted to purchase the book for distribution by their companies; again Little, Brown said no. In fact, paperback rights have never been sold. Foreign publishers rushed to buy translation rights, and these were sold so that the book would be available throughout the world. *Human Sexual Response* has been now published in ten languages.

Masters and Johnson were beset by the press in St. Louis. There were such pressures for information on both the authors and the publisher that finally, at Virginia Johnson's suggestion, science writers were invited to Boston in small groups to talk with the authors. Publication had turned into a news story that needed covering. News conferences, which many distinguished science writers from all over the country attended, were held at the Ritz-Carlton Hotel early in April, 1966. Everyone invited to the sessions had been provided with a set of proofs before coming to Boston. The writers had done their homework carefully, and with a good understanding of the book they were able to ask a wide range of important questions and to react in an unbiased and unsensational manner. Masters and Johnson say that journalists have always been extremely fair and helpful to them.

In talking of press conferences, Mrs. Johnson commented, "People from the press are required to deal in a world of reality, and what we were saying made sense to them. They were very receptive." Masters and Johnson feel the responsible news coverage speeded the process of cultural change and put them into perspective as changers of the times and as part of the times. In *Human Sexual Response* they had put together pretty much all that was known about sexual functioning, and the members of the press, with their open attitudes, helped to interpret and to present this information in a way the general public could readily understand.

The sizable first printing of *Human Sexual Response* was sold out three days after publication on April 19, 1966. Even though it was a medical book, it rose quickly to number two position on *The New York Times* nonfiction best-seller list. (One quipster suggested that it was "the cleanest book on the list.") There were still some cries from the intellectual community, along the lines of the Farber attack in *Commentary,* that Masters and Johnson were taking the romance out of lovemaking, and that presentation of their material would lead to a world of sex without privacy, tenderness, or naturalness. Malcolm Muggeridge, for example, declared, "This surely is the apogee of the sexual revolution, the ultimate expression of the cult of the orgasm—the American Dream at last fulfilled."

Many complained that the book was hard to understand and that it was written in turgid prose with convoluted syntax. Reviewing it in the New York *Post*, Max Lerner wrote: "They are committed scientists. Hence perhaps the book's language—oh, the language —which is so severely technical and barbarous as to make Kinsey seem a light essayist."

Most of the public took news of the book, its contents and its methods of study in stride. A new day allowing scientific study of sex was about to begin. This was a far cry from the furor raised by Congressman Louis Heller of Brooklyn when Alfred C. Kinsey's *Sexual Behavior in the Human Female* appeared. At that time Heller wanted the book banned from the mails because he felt Kinsey's group was "hurling the insult of the century against our mothers, wives, daughters, and sisters." This was not the only attack on Kinsey; there were many, and Kinsey had only asked people questions about sex. He hadn't watched them in the act! Times had changed.

There were still many protesters, as Masters and Johnson expected there would be. Mrs. Johnson commented, "It's a wonderful thing to be able to sense well ahead of your time what needs to be done; it's another to try to get everybody to accept you instantly. People have to grow accustomed to new concepts. They have visceral reactions that have nothing to do with their intellectual capacity." A number of physicians and spirited citizens wrote letters canceling their subscriptions to *Time* when that magazine ran a story on Masters and Johnson. One doctor complained about "the indisputable poor taste" of the magazine for printing the story, and another asked to be spared any more of these "Masters-pieces." A father of college students wrote that *Time* had reached "the bottom in the pail of filth."

Many serious thinkers in medicine and the behavioral sciences reacted quickly saying that Masters and Johnson had made original and significant contributions to sexology. Frank A. Beach wrote in *Scientific American*:

> Viewed as a series of investigations into the functions of the reproductive system, the work reported in this book can be most meaningfully compared to the pioneering observations and experiments of William Beaumont, Walter B. Cannon and others in connection with the physiology of the digestive system. There are obvious similarities to Beaumont's brilliant discoveries concerning the movement of food through the stomach which were facilitated by the opportunity to obtain samples directly through an opening in the stomach of one of his subjects. The present work is also comparable to Cannon's classic experiment demonstrating that the physical basis of hunger pangs in contraction of the stomach muscles, a demonstration made possible by recording the pressure changes in a small balloon that had been swallowed and then inflated to fill the stomach's interior. Cannon's procedure in comparing his subject's report of hunger pangs with the mechanical record of stomach activity is directly comparable to Masters and Johnson's correlation between their subjects' reports of sexual orgasm.

Almost all the editors of medical periodicals lauded the book and its findings, one going so far as to say that he was sure Masters would be "revered for his scientific guts." Reviewers praised Masters and Johnson for their courage in undertaking the work. The editor of the *Journal of the American Medical Association* commented:

> To some sex is the ultimate area of privacy, and hence not appropriate for study and evaluation. No scientific criteria can justify such a conclusion. . . . We may look upon Masters' investigation as a natural and inevitable consequence of changing cultural involvement.
>
> Today, many people sincerely feel that the present atmosphere of frankness and public concern over sexual matters is basically amoral and destructive. Nevertheless, even the most critical should admit that, if we are able to free some individuals from neurotic guilt feelings about sex and if we can utilize scientific research to stabilize even a few apparently unsuccessful marriages, some good had been served. None of these admirable designs is achievable through ignorance.

Another reviewer said, "This reviewer in the shadow of Victorian thinking could not imagine a study of sexuality of normal men and women under laboratory conditions." He then went on to say that even so, he recognized the vision and courage of the investigators and the research population: "With certainty the authors have forever disposed of some of the folklore, fantasies and half-truths which have contributed to the pseudo-science of sexuality as evolved in a Victorian society."

Don Jackson, professor of Psychiatry at Stanford

University, and a nationally known authority, commented on the opposition to the book from within the medical community:

> Many physicians, despite the nature of their profession, are the victims of this culture and are therefore prudes; they resent Masters' investigations as much as if he had taken religion to task. It is not uncommon for physicans to ask: "Is he happily married?" and "What does Mrs. Johnson look like?" But what relevance do these (and similar) questions have to Masters' competence as a medical researcher? Would a colleague inquire how many surgical procedures DeBakey has had performed on himself, or whether he ever suffered from a broken heart?

Even several board members of the Sex Information and Education Council of the United States (SIECUS) voiced reservations about the propriety of the method of the study from psychological, moral, or religious points of view. All agreed, however, that the findings themselves were valuable. (Since publication of *Human Sexual Response,* Masters has been asked to serve as a member of the Board of Directors of SIECUS, and has accepted.) As Harold Lief wrote in *SIECUS Newsletter*:

> At any rate, even if the research methods should offend some value systems, the observations recorded by Masters and Johnson have such tremendous potential for the improved medical treatment of sexual inadequacy, for sex education that would lead to mature personalities, and for future research, that this should outweigh any possible affront to some sensibilities.

Colin Hindley, a biologist at the University of London, captured the feeling of the times nicely when he said of the book, "If we are inclined to regard sexual union as something so sacrosanct that it should not be open to investigation, we should remember that a similar view was taken regarding the stars in Galileo's day."

During the years since the publication of *Human Sexual Response* there has been no serious scientific challenge to it. The findings reported in it have become widely accepted. In assessing acceptance with the medical community today, Masters says:

> It is inevitably true that medical training engenders a healthy suspicion—and that is good. Findings should be considered wrong until they can be proved right. This takes years. We have passed from the black area in terms of acceptance of *Human Sexual Response* to a gray area, a middle ground. That is the way it should be. I think we are handicapped some because the techniques we originated have been taken and bastardized by a lot of quacks. This still tends to make a certain section on medicine think we are quacks too. Until they read our work in depth they should be skeptical.

Many critics charged that the book was being bought by the public for titillation. If there was some truth in this, it was far from the prime reason. The authors had deliberately tried to take out or change anything in the book that might be misconstrued as pornographic, and, as one Catholic publication aptly commented, "For those seeking pornography, much more stimulating material is available at considerably less cost than the ten dollars for the Masters-Johnson report."

People mostly bought the book for information. This became quickly apparent; just after publication Masters and Johnson began receiving letters which eventually numbered in the thousands. Eighty percent were from people asking for help with sexual problems. Perhaps ten percent were hate letters, the rest praise or encouragement.

Many people also wrote long, unhappy letters to the publisher, ordering the book and detailing, in page after page, their own sexual sufferings. All these letters were sent to Dr. Masters and Mrs. Johnson for replies. They would not diagnose or treat anyone's problem by mail, but tried always to refer the person to a competent counselor near his own home. Sometimes they arranged to have the couple come to St. Louis for treatment. It is difficult to convey to anyone who has never seen these desperate letters the seriousness and enormity of sexual problems in America. Letters to Masters and Johnson imploring them for help even went so far as to offer payment—any amount—for advice. Some not so serious inquiries also came to Little, Brown. A major Hollywood film studio called to buy movie rights to the book. The caller was asked if he had actually read it. He admitted he had not, but said he understood that it was a very good story.

A New York theater agent phoned to inquire if the musical-comedy rights for the book were available. An American pornographer living in Europe wrote lengthy letters begging the publisher to let him handle all of the European rights for *Human Sexual Response*. His plan was to work the book into a series of still photographs and action movies, and he assured Little, Brown that he really knew how to sell books outside of the usual bookselling channels. Needless to say, these and other offers of similar nature were declined.

After publication of *Human Sexual Response* life changed dramatically for Masters and Johnson. They were internationally recognized for the contributions they had made. The book was widely commented on throughout the world. Before publication lecture invitations were frequent, but afterward, the number of requests was all but overwhelming. They went on a series of one-night stands that would have done in the hardiest traveler. They said they could hardly tell where they were without looking at the hotel matches. In 1967 they were away from St. Louis lecturing for four months; in 1968 for four and a half months. "We had to appear in a variety of places and before a variety of disciplines and let people know we didn't have two heads," said Masters. They admit it was a nightmarish grind, and vowed they would never do it again. About the travel Masters commented, "I don't know how much good we did, but I know we neutralized a lot of the bad, and we got an education by going around."

Their reception around the country was usually good, although they did meet hostile audiences from time to time. As a lecture team they are especially effective. Masters handles the medical aspects; Mrs. Johnson, who thinks of herself as a "people person," gets through to individuals of all kinds in every audience, while competently and perceptively explaining the psychologic aspects of the work. They have talked before thousands of people. In looking back, they find it is hard to assess just how much they educated their audiences, whether professional or general. Mrs. Johnson believes, "We made people more comfortable with the subject. I don't think we really educated. You must make sexual material palatable because so many sexual facts are against individual beliefs. Many in the audiences were so busy contending with their own 'visceral clutch' that they didn't really hear a lot of what we said."

Whether the audience was professional or student, the questions people asked were everywhere very much the same. Neither group had accurate information about sexual functioning. In fact, students were apt to be more free about asking questions than were professionals, especially doctors accompanied by their wives. The physicians did not want their wives to be aware of their ignorance and were hesitant to ask questions. Masters and Johnson gradually developed techniques of opening discussions with such groups. One device they employed when speaking before a professional, middle-aged audience was to pose a sample question in a way to divert the attention of people in the audience away from themselves. One of them might say, for example, after asking for questions and getting no response, "Your son, if he is representative of most young people with whom we speak, would want to ask about the size of the penis and whether a larger one would make him a better lover." Or, "Girls your daughter's age frequently ask how often should people have intercourse when they are married." Of course, these are the questions people of all ages want to ask. Often wives would ask the first questions, and the physicians would follow with their own inquiries. Many receptive doctors wanted to know how they could apply the Foundation's findings to their own practices.

Masters and Johnson completed eleven years of work with patients in treatment before writing their second book, *Human Sexual Inadequacy*. Their final statistics could not be gathered and assimilated until late 1969, just a few months before they began writing. The entire book was completed in six weeks, with Masters and Johnson again setting work schedules for themselves that would have exhausted most people. They promised themselves and their publishers, Little, Brown, that they would have their manuscript ready on January 1, 1970, and they did. As Mrs. Johnson said, "Bill has never been known to miss a deadline."

PART II

UNDERSTANDING HUMAN SEXUAL INADEQUACY

CHAPTER 7

Rapid Treatment of Human Sexual Inadequacy: Principles of the Program

The rapid treatment program described by Masters and Johnson in *Human Sexual Inadequacy* is unique in the history of medicine. Based on fifteen years' study of sexually functional subjects in the laboratory and eleven years of clinical work with sexually inadequate people, it is no longer experimental. Many patients have now been followed up five years after the initial two-week therapy program. There simply is no program to compare with it in terms of time span or data accumulated. In applying what they learned in the laboratory to the treatment of sexual dysfunction, Masters and Johnson have, in addition, developed an undertstanding of the psychology of sexual response.

Discussing the validation of their work, Dr. Masters approached this uniqueness as a problem. "Our clinical work, just like our laboratory work, isn't worth anything until somebody has repeated it. We have been as hard on ourselves as we could, statistically. We want to be sure that anybody can go out with any sort of training and reduplicate our eighty percent success results and write a paper saying, 'In St. Louis they don't know what they're doing; we can do ninety percent.' That would be great."

Concepts Underlying the Treatment Program

> Sociocultural deprivation and ignorance of sexual physiology, rather than psychiatric or medical illness, constitute the etiologic background for most sexual dysfunction.[1]

That our attitudes and our ignorance, rather than any mental or physical illness, are responsible for most of our sexual problems, is a basic assumption underlying the treatment program. The implication is that a short-term educational effort combined with supportive psychotherapy is likely to be a reasonable approach to the treatment of sexual inadequacy. This kind of therapy is what Masters and Johnson attempt to do.

A contrary view about the cause of sexual dysfunction prevails in our American culture. Most people, including physicians, think that sexual problems are always a symptom of some deep-lying psychiatric illness. For those who can afford it, the traditional treatment has been long-term psychotherapy or psychoanalysis. For most people, however, there has been no treatment. The family doctor's answer to questions about impotence, premature ejaculation, frigidity, and so on, has been, "I can't do anything about it." And this is true! Masters and Johnson's new book has now changed that outlook. They have shown that there now is a treatment program which will work for many people, that the program

---

[1] *HSI*, p. 21.

can be relatively brief, and that it can be taught to other therapists.

The treatment program itself is a series of educational and psychotherapeutic talk sessions between the therapists and the patients. The therapists also give step-by-step instructions to the patients regarding the physical aspects of sexual activity. These instructions are carried out by the couple in private, and what happens in the couple's private sessions is discussed by the patients and therapists in the next talk session. The present chapter describes the assumptions, ideas, and therapeutic methods upon which the Masters and Johnson treatment program is based. Chapter 8 is a résumé of instructions given to all patients in the first four days of the treatment program, and subsequent chapters detail the treatment of specific problems.

The Relationship Between the Partners Is the Patient

> . . . there is no such thing as an uninvolved partner in any marriage in which there is some form of sexual inadequacy.[2]

The inevitable frustrations and misunderstandings built up between a husband and wife over the period of one partner's inadequacy usually have damaged the relationship between them. This vital problem cannot be dealt with if the dysfunctional partner is in therapy alone. Masters and Johnson, therefore, insist that both husband and wife participate in the treatment program.

Another problem arises if an individual with a sexual problem is treated alone. The partner of that person is

---
[2] *HSI*, p. 2.

left completely in the dark about what is happening in treatment, and may accidentally or purposefully interfere with the therapy because really both partners are emotionally involved in the problem. For example, if a woman is married to an impotent man who is in psychotherapy, she never knows what she should do or not do next. If she shows sexual interest, will she frighten her husband by seeming to demand sexual performance? If she represses her sexual feeling, will she hurt him by seeming lack of interest? If there is sexual opportunity, should she be simply compliant or should she take some initiative?

Even if the wife knew what to do to help, she might not be able to manage it because of the damage to the marital relationship over the years. Suppose the husband's therapist tried to instruct the couple by giving directions for both to the husband. Involved in a troubled relationship, with her side of the story unheard, is a wife likely to be able to cooperate even if she intends to do so?

Sexual interaction requires the involvement of two people. Isolating one partner in therapy often breaks down whatever communication existed between them before. Masters and Johnson have established that it is the relationship which must be treated if sexual function is to be restored. This is why both partners must be present in therapy. They stress that when a relationship has disintegrated totally or when there is profound disinterest from either partner, therapy is useless.

The Dual-Sex Therapy Team. All the results of treatment reported in *Human Sexual Inadequacy* were obtained by two therapists, one of each sex, working with each couple. Masters' statement that he could not understand sexual functioning without having a woman to interpret female response for him must be stressed. This concept was carried over into the treatment program where several other advantages of a male-female therapy team became apparent.

When there is a dual-sex therapy team, the husband and wife each have a "friend in court" and "an interpreter" of the same sex who can support and explain that person's point of view during the talk sessions. For example, if a man is the "strong silent type," it really would be necessary to have another man present who could verbalize for him feelings which he cannot express, and who could, in addition, explain unemotionally to the wife the fears, pressures, and anxieties that weigh upon the sexually inadequate man. Likewise, a tense excitable wife needs another woman to express logically and reasonably what she is trying to tell her husband and possibly the male cotherapist too. The dual-sex therapy teams are an immeasurable aid to keeping the record straight, avoiding misinterpretations and misunderstandings, and guiding the couple through the barriers set up by their problem.

Another distinct advantage of the dual-sex team is that it avoids what Masters and Johnson have named "the feeling of ganging-up." If a male therapist is treating a sexually dysfunctional couple, the wife often feels that the two-to-one sex ratio of the group works to her disadvantage. A critical appraisal or a set of instructions directed to the wife may give her the feeling of being overwhelmed because of the unbalanced sex ratio. Besides, there is no one to explain to the wife facts of female sexuality about which men are generally unaware. There is also no one to help her if she can't get her ideas through to the two men. The same problem would arise in reverse if the therapist were a female.

Use of dual-sex teams also greatly reduces the possibility of getting biased information from the patients. As Masters and Johnson put it, a woman patient usually will tell a male therapist

> . . . first what she wants him to know; second, what she thinks he wants to know or can understand; and not until a third, ultimately persuasive attempt has been made can she consistently be relied upon to present material as it is or as it really appears to her.[3]

If there is another woman present, a woman patient will be much more likely to tell it the first time the way she really sees it. A female therapist taking a history from a male patient is at the same disadvantage or possibly even a worse one because it is not culturally acceptable for a man to unburden himself to a woman. With cotherapists of both sexes present during interviews, the social rigmarole performed to impress the other sex is minimized.

Readers who are familiar with psychotherapeutic techniques will understand the term "transference." Simply put, "transference" refers to a transfer of positive or negative feelings felt by the patient for some important person in his life (usually a mother, father, husband, or wife) from this person to the therapist. In other words, the patient comes to feel toward the therapist the way he does toward his mother, father, husband, wife, or whoever the most relevant figure happens to be. This naturally occurring phenomenon is one of the most useful tools in psychotherapy because it allows the patient to work through all his ancient hurts and dis-

---

[3] *HSI*, p. 6.

appointments, with the therapist serving as the understanding parent or spouse he may not have had before.

Masters and Johnson feel that allowing transference of a positive sexual nature to occur between a patient and a therapist has no place in a program of brief therapy for sexual dysfunction. The effect of having a husband or wife develop a special affinity for a therapist of the opposite sex, thus replacing the mate, is destructive to the marital relationship. It may open emotional communicative channels between the therapist and patient, but at the same time it closes the channels between the patient and spouse. This is a disaster because success in sex therapy is dependent upon communication between the sex partners.

Dual-sex therapy teams have a tremendous advantage in dealing with this kind of transference. If the wife, for example, begins to pay attention exclusively to the male cotherapist, he will then direct all his questions and responses to the husband, while the female cotherapist deals with all matters relating to the wife. It does not take long for the wife to realize that she will not be allowed to develop a special relationship with the male cotherapist.

The final advantage of having two people on the therapy team is that both necessary medical disciplines are immediately available to the patients. So far, teams have been composed of a physician and a psychologist. Having a physician on the team means that the couple does not have to be embarrassed by outside referral for the necessary physical and laboratory examinations. The psychologist, of course, contributes the vital know-how about why people behave and feel the way they do. Both members of the team must be knowledgeable about sexual functioning, secure in their own feelings about themselves as men and women, and completely at ease about discussing sexual matters with other people. Unfortunately, there are too many people doing sex counseling today who cannot meet these criteria.

That Masters and Johnson's methods can be taught is proved by the success of their colleagues, Sallie S. Schumacher and Richard H. Spitz. After working with patients for only one year, their treatment results vary by only ten percent from Masters and Johnson's.

Therapists now take turns working with each other, so that Dr. Schumacher works with Dr. Masters and Dr. Spitz with Mrs. Johnson some of the time. Mrs. Johnson has commented that this keeps everyone from getting stale.

Patients are told before they come to St. Louis that they will be assigned to a therapy team upon arrival. There is excellent patient acceptance of the new therapists and of the fact that the founders cannot treat all the patients who come to the Foundation.

General Therapeutic Procedures

The Silent Partner. The dual-sex "team" is a team in every sense. It does not work by hit-or-miss interaction. There is always one partner calling the signals during the talk sessions, but surprisingly, the cotherapist who is not talking at any given moment is the one who is in charge.

The way it works, say Masters and Johnson, is that "the silent partner really acts as the coach of the team." The coach listens carefully to the discussion and watches for nonverbal clues as well, while the other cotherapist's attention is mostly focused on talking and asking questions. When it is necessary to change the topic under discussion or to explain something more clearly, the roles change. The silent partner, whose attention has been free to observe the patient's reaction and to catch nuances of the discussion, takes over, leading the discussion in the direction he feels it should go. It is up to the silent partner to evaluate whether the patients are accepting or rejecting the material under discussion and to spot areas which are particularly distressing. The cotherapists also change roles when it is necessary for a man or a woman therapist to present particular material.

The advantage of having an observer is enormous because no one person can direct a discussion and attend to all the other signals as well. Masters says, "One is concentrating on talking and the other is concentrating on nonverbal communication. For example, if I were taking a history from a man, and he did not want to talk about his homosexual background—he wanted to fool me—he might fool me. But he might be giving himself away to the cotherapist sitting over there watching the expression on his face. The observer therapist would say after he left, 'Look, let's go back over that again. I think there's something there.' The advantage of the observer is that he can concentrate on watching the patient's facial expression, his body tension, his hands, his total presence."

"Holding Up a Mirror." The key technique that the dual-sex teams employ is called "reflective teaching." During the psychotherapy sessions, the cotherapists make it possible for the marital partners to see themselves as they are. They restate for the couple in an objective, unemotional way what their problems are, how they are hurting each other, and how they fail to communicate with each other. No judgments are made; a "mirror" of their own behavior is simply held up for the patients to look at. This technique usually makes it possible for the patients to accept constructive criticism because for the first time they understand the destructive elements in their own behavior toward each other and toward themselves. Masters and Johnson describe their approach to this teaching role as "a bit formal." For example, they never address patients by their first names because they feel that the patients need a somewhat authoritarian role.

Once the patients can accept criticism and instruction, they are ready to allow themselves to think and feel about sex as the natural process it is. Masters and Johnson point out that sexual functioning is the only physiologic process which a person can deny voluntarily and which individuals do sacrifice for any number of reasons —religious, personal, or simply as a matter of convenience. Everyone rejects sexual stimuli when he feels that the circumstances are inappropriate. Sexually dysfunctional people, however, have taken their sexuality completely from its naturally occurring context. Instead of allowing the physiologic sexual responses to occur at least some of the time, they have blocked them off altogether. The "mirror," or reflective technique, helps the patients to see these barriers and remove them.

Masters and Johnson have pointed out that one of the most damaging barriers to sexual stimulation set up by a dysfunctional individual is the assumption of "a spectator role." Instead of getting involved, instead of forgetting everything else and letting sexual arousal happen naturally, this person mentally sets himself apart and observes his own responses. A person may assume the spectator role because he or she is afraid of failing to respond. In any case, it is a most unnatural situation, one which blocks the reception of sexual stimulation. The jobs of explaining about spectator roles and "holding the mirror" for these people are best done by the cotherapist of the same sex. Getting a patient to quit being a spectator is a big step in restoring sex for an individual to a naturally occurring function.

Abolishing Goal-oriented Performance. One of the main tasks of the cotherapists is to remove the pressure to "produce, perform, and achieve" from the patients. "Other therapy has usually been directed at teaching the individual to do something," declares Masters. "We insist he doesn't have to *do* anything! All we really do is remove him from the spectator role first—we're banking on mother nature. We let her run the show. Nobody really appreciated that sex is a natural function until we went into the laboratory and found it out. We had no concept of this either. We always thought we should be teaching something. It just isn't so. A man is born with the ability to achieve an erection. The first time he had one he didn't think about it, he found himself with it."

A man's fear of failing in the sex act is the most effective barrier to sexual stimulation possible. The concern of a man who has had erective failures intensifies it every time he approaches a woman sexually. He is completely distracted by the thought that he won't have an erection, or that it won't be hard enough to insert his penis. What he doesn't face is that worrying about the involuntary process of getting an erection, is worse than useless. As Masters and Johnson have said many times, a man cannot will an erection. At the same time, the partner of this man has her own fears. She worries not only about his ability, but also she fears that she will do or say the wrong things, making his problem worse. The anxiety engendered by these fears makes it impossible for this couple to relax and to become involved with each other in a sexually stimulating way. They are concerned with the achievement of a result rather than with participation and involvement in a spontaneous and natural process.

The woman who cannot have orgasm has performance fears too. She fears that something is wrong with her, that she is not attractive to her husband. To this situation, the husband is likely to contribute his own anxieties. Our cultural demand on the male to "do something" makes him feel responsible for her nonorgasmic state. He asks himself why he can't satisfy her and inevitably worries so much about his own performance that he can't allow himself the intensely pleasurable personal involvement that would lead to climax for his wife.

The first step in the removal of performance fears is for the therapists to forbid at the outset of the treatment program any sexual activity not instigated at their direction. The educative reflective process designed to help the couple understand their fears is begun, and then the couple is led in a step-by-step process to mutual and pleasurable sexual involvement. This process is described in the next chapter and in the chapters on specific sexual problems. Never is it suggested during the early stages of therapy that the couple go all the way toward sexual fulfillment at once. Sexual responsiveness is acquired little by little, with success in the beginning steps used as building blocks for progress in later phases.

The Cotherapists as a Communication Catalyst. According to Masters and Johnson, the most important role of the cotherapists is to get communication going between the dysfunctional partners. At first, communication is primarily between the patients and the therapists.

But after a few days, the therapists encourage direct discussion between the patients themselves. Evidence of therapeutic progress is the decreasing necessity for participation by the cotherapists in the talk sessions. When the patients are communicating with each other, and when there is personal rapport between them, the therapists can proceed in the treatment of the couple's specific problem.

Masters and Johnson comment, "Most husbands and wives want to make therapy work. Say they've been married fifteen years; they have two or three children; the man has a career; they have a place in the community. Both would like to make a go of it, but really they can't. In a sense they have long since given up, but they would like to think that therapy can work, and so they come to St. Louis. After a decade or so of being roommates, they've talked a lot, but they have never really said anything to each other. When we hold up the 'mirror' for them, give them back verbally what they have said to us, they look at each other as though they didn't know each other and are just seeing each other in focus for the first time. For about forty-eight hours it spills out, and we let it. It's a wonderful catharsis. After that time, if they are still sounding off, we intercede. We tell them you cannot win in the future if you are going to project the future in terms of the past. We encourage them to go on and not wallow in their past, and most respond and move ahead."

Who Comes to the Foundation for Treatment

All the couples accepted by the Foundation for treatment are referred from physicians, psychologists, social workers, or clergymen. For the first three years of the treatment program, from 1959 to 1962, Masters and Johnson stipulated that patients must have had a minimum of six months of psychotherapy with failure to reverse symptoms before being accepted by the Foundation. Eventually, they decided they could not know how cooperative the patient had been or how good the psychotherapy had been, so they substituted the requirement that an individual must be referred by someone with training in medicine or a behavioral science or by a clergyman. This practice has been followed for the past eight years, and it has worked well.

Many people in the medical and behavioral specialties have referred themselves, skewing the sample of couples toward the higher educational and socioeconomic levels. Usually the educated and affluent in any society learn about new things first and have the money to buy them. That a high percentage of the Foundation's patients fit these categories is not surprising. Other investigators have shown that persons in lower socioeconomic groups do not usually seek treatment of sexual disorders even when free care is available. It is not known whether this means they have no problems, whether pride prevents the men from seeking treatment and they restrain the women, or whether there is a communication barrier between these people and the available therapists. Masters and Johnson say they have not had enough experience with less privileged groups to comment on the situation, although some blue-collar workers have come for therapy. It is questionable whether the rapid-treatment program would work for people at all socioeconomic and educational levels. Because their patients are well motivated, usually well-educated people who are screened and then referred, the Foundation does not see a cross section of the population; again they admit they just do not know.

During their first years of care, from 1959 to 1964, patients were not charged a fee because Masters and Johnson were just developing their clinical techniques. Beginning in 1965, twenty-five percent of the patients received free care, twenty-five percent paid adjusted fees, and fifty percent paid full fees. Full fee is $2,500 for the two-week program and five years of follow-up consultation. The patients pay their own living expenses in St. Louis. Even with an adjusted fee schedule, patients have tended to be middle class or above. Although patients have been drawn from various racial, ethnic, and religious groups, Masters and Johnson are quick to concede that they do not have anything like a true crosscultural sampling.

The referring sources provide valuable background information about the patients, and the Foundation reports to the referring sources about their patients' progress. There is an effort to screen out people whose relationship has deteriorated so far that they are totally alienated from each other. In such instances therapy is most likely to be a waste of time. Although psychotic patients are not accepted, people are referred to the Foundation for treatment of a sexual difficulty which is part of a larger psychologic problem. These people return to their original therapist after the two-week program.

Patients who come to St. Louis for the two weeks are asked to make no other commitments during that time. Isolated from their ordinary business, social, and family contacts, they have the opportunity to communicate with each other without interruptions and are free to participate seven days a week in the rapid-treatment program.

St. Louis residents are asked to allow three weeks for therapy, since they continue to live at home during treatment and are subject to family and business distractions. Foundation personnel also make special efforts to see to it that the patients enjoy a vacation while they are in St. Louis. Information about restaurants, theaters, lecures, concerts, sports, and places of interest to visit is made available.

When the patients agree to come to St. Louis, they are also asked to commit themselves to be available for follow-up study for five years if their short-term therapy is successful. If the two-week program is unsuccessful, Masters and Johnson try to refer the patients to some other therapist or program which may be more suitable for that particular couple. They do not try to follow treatment failures because they feel it would not be in the patients' best interest. Patients who are successful in the two-week program agree to be in touch with Masters and Johnson periodically for five years, usually by telephone. In this way, the long-term results of the treatment program can be evaluated, and the patients have available the continuing advice and counsel of the therapists.

CHAPTER 8

Rapid Treatment of Human Sexual Inadequacy: The Daily Program

Day One

Two writers going to St. Louis to interview Masters and Johnson were riding in a cab from the St. Louis airport to the Foundation. "How would we feel right now," asked one, "if we were a couple coming for treatment?" Anxious, angry, jittery, afraid, hopeful—they decided the first day would be a difficult time.

Foundation personnel are aware of this problem, and the initial procedures are planned to put the couple at ease and to insure their privacy. The Foundation is located at 4910 Forest Park Boulevard where other doctors also have offices. Masters and Johnson find this an advantageous arrangement because the patients do not feel conspicuous. Feelings and attitudes on arrival are generally as varied as the individual patients, except, Dr. Masters says, "Every married couple, if they are speaking at all, will try to have intercourse the night before they see us, just to see if they can. They get here and inevitably they go to bed together."

Tensions can accumulate between the time the couple

makes the appointment to visit St. Louis and the start of therapy. "This is why we are very sad that there is a time lag of three to five months in most instances," Mrs. Johnson says. "We are working with the wife's menstrual cycle, children's school schedules, professional demands on the couple, and our schedule too." "If we had more therapists we could see people sooner," adds Masters. "Sometimes, because the delay is long, people talk themselves out of treatment. Some patients are so fearful on arrival that they are very defensive at first. Others, once they have made the commitment, are so pleased to reach someone who will help that they are relaxed and open from the start of the first interview."

The Initial Interview. Every newly arrived couple meets with both cotherapists for the first time in a brief interview during which their commitments to the program and the procedure for the first few days are explained.

The couple is told first that all therapy sessions are recorded. Microphones in the interview areas are all visible, but there is no recording equipment present. All conversations are recorded by equipment in a central security room, and the tapes are stored there. This system has advantages for both patients and therapists. The time and energy of the cotherapists are conserved, and the tapes provide a foolproof way of retrieving material should that be necessary. Having the interviews proceed without note-taking leaves the cotherapists free to concentrate on the interview itself. The patients' privacy is protected because there is no need to dictate and type records. Masters and Johnson say that the loyalty and discretion of their staff with regard to patients' privacy is remarkable. A woman who had done housekeeping for the Foundation for fifteen years came to Dr. Masters' office one day and inquired, "Dr. Masters, I have some relatives coming to visit this week—is it all right if I tell them where I work?"

The format of the next few days is explained to the patients at this initial session. They are told that immediately after the interview they will separate, and the husband will give a history to the male cotherapist, while the wife relates her history to the female cotherapist. It is explained that the next day they will change about, the wife talking with the male cotherapist and the husband with the female cotherapist. The physical examination and laboratory evaluations scheduled for the third day are described briefly, and the couple is also told that on the third day there will be a session known as the roundtable, at which both partners and both cotherapists are present. The patients are asked not to discuss any of the history-taking sessions until the roundtable. Obviously, this method is an inducement for people to present themselves and their stories honestly right from the start.

Often patients come to the Foundation with the mistaken idea that they will be expected to participate in the laboratory physiology studies. No sexually dysfunctional patient who comes to the Foundation for therapy would ever be permitted to be a study subject. A therapist would never suggest to a patient that he perform sexually for laboratory study when his sexual performance is inadequate.

The Foundation concept that no partner is uninvolved when there is a problem of sexual dysfunction is emphasized to married patients. They are told that they can be accepted as patients only if they agree with this concept and thereby pledge their involvement in the program and promise their cooperation.

Finally, the first physical direction is given to the couple: they are asked not to have intercourse or to participate in any other sexual activity until told to do so by a therapist.

The initial interview always takes place in the office of the female cotherapist so that at the end, when it is time to separate for the first history-taking, it is the men who stand up to leave. The cotherapists have discovered that a man is relatively at ease taking leave of his wife, but that it is difficult for wives to do the same.

The First History-taking Interview. Having the two women and the two men first talk with each other in private leads patients to identify personally with the therapist of the same sex. This therapist becomes the patient's "friend" and "interpreter" during the talk sessions. To begin the first history-taking interview, the therapist usually asks the patient, "Why are you here?" or "What's the trouble?"—thus eliciting a brief description of the presenting complaint. Mrs. Johnson explains, "This gives you a sense of the patient before you have imposed your impression on him. The patient is put in the position of immediately having to reveal himself."

After the patient has described his problem, the therapist follows by asking how the patient has dealt with the problem so far, what he thinks normal sexual functioning is, and what he thinks appropriate male and female roles are in marriage. The purpose of these questions is to define the problem and to assess the likelihood of a cure, taking into consideration the severity of the dysfunction and the state of the marriage relationship.

The patients are asked very specific questions about their sexual functioning. For example, a woman might be asked whether she ever has orgasm, and if so, to describe the physical feeling of it. Not only does this kind of questioning provide information, but it also gives the therapist the opportunity to create, by manner and tone of voice, an atmosphere in which sex can be talked about comfortably.

During the first interview the basic chronology of the patient's life is put in the record. Questions are asked about the patient's childhood—when and where he was born; was the home broken by death or divorce; did the family move a lot; was religion important; what was the atmosphere of the home—was it warm, was it cold; was sex ever discussed; did the parents get on well; were there brothers and sisters; were there friends. Within this framework questions are asked about sex: When did the patient first try masturbating; how frequently did he do it; was he ever caught; does he masturbate now; does he summon specific fantasies during masturbation or during intercourse; does he dream about sex; as a child did the patient ever try any sexual activity with another person; did the patient ever watch anyone else having sex.

Questions about adolescence center around school, the patient's relations with family and friends and the beginning of sexual activity—to which parent did the patient feel closer; did he get on well with parents; was the patient a good student; how far did he go in school; what was the family's position in the community; were there any special school friends; when did menstruation or nocturnal emissions ("wet dreams") begin; had this been discussed before at home; did the patient have dates; what kind of sexual activity was there on dates; was there genital play; was there intercourse; describe the first time—with what frequency did it recur; was it pleasurable, worrisome; was the patient ever seen engaging in sexual activity and punished; was there homosexual experience.

The patient's adult life prior to marriage is explored as well—were there engagements; why terminated; what were the most meaningful relationships (positive or negative) during this time; were there friends; was there homosexual activity.

As the history unfolds, past events or influences that have erotic meaning for the patient begin to emerge. The meanings given by the patient to these events and influences form his sexual value system. It becomes apparent whether the patient gives sexual functioning an honorable place in his scheme of things, and under what circumstances sexual functioning is allowed. Episodic sexual success in the past does not necessarily mean success in the future, but still a detailed exploration of successful past experiences may show what the patient's sexual requirements are. Knowing what they are can be a person's first step in the right direction.

All the basic statistics of the patient's marriage or marriages are collected—length of courtship, duration, number of children, premarital activity, extramarital activity. Attention is directed specifically to potentially significant areas—what was the courtship like; what was then attractive about the fiancé(e); is that quality still present; what were the patient's expectations about sex; were there difficulties on the honeymoon; how frequent was intercourse during the first months of marriage; is there communication between the partners about what they like sexually; do the partners share confidences; do they get along well with family members; do they have a sense of humor; what habits or behavior patterns of the other partner are displeasing sexually; how often does intercourse occur now; what circumstances influence lovemaking most; who chooses the time; is there a preference for a particular time or situation; what is missing now in the way of the spouse's behavior or attitude; what is positive about the spouse's attitudes and behavior; is the other partner a good parent.

Special focusing on the senses—touch, sight, hearing, smell—is important in the treatment program because the ability to associate sexual arousal with various sensual perceptions is important for sexual functioning. First the therapist gathers some basic information about the patient's sensual feelings: Does the patient feel attractive; would he like to change something about himself; what is his best attribute as a person; what is the patient's greatest contribution to a social situation; how would he describe his sexual identity; is he happy with it.

The patient's attitudes and responses with regard to touch are explored carefully because of the special importance of this sense to sexual expression: Does the patient like to touch, to explore surfaces to see if they are smooth, patterned or rough, to explore the body of his partner in the same way; does the partner accept this touch; does the patient find himself petting small children or animals; does he use body contact to express feelings—if so, when and what sort; does the patient ever find touching irritating, embarrassing or intolerable; what does the patient think of as the most sexually stimulating kind of touch; does he like to be held close after intercourse; what happens when he wants body contact and is ignored; what does the patient like most—the expression of feeling through touch and body contact or intercourse; what is the nicest kind of touch the patient recalls from childhood; who gave it.

Although touch may be most significant, the other

senses have a role which is also explored: Does the patient think his partner looks attractive; was this a primary factor in the choice; does the patient like the spouse to be well dressed; does either wear special kinds of clothing during lovemaking and sexual activity; does the patient enjoy watching his partner; is the patient especially aware of odors; which ones are pleasant; is the pleasure related to something; are any odors discomforting and why; has awareness of odors changed since marriage; are certain kinds of odors more masculine and others more feminine; what odor about the patient's home pleases him most; does the patient enjoy the smell of his marital partner's body—without scented products or with them; does the patient like the smell of a clean body; is he particularly aware of odors and perfume of other people; when the patient's partner is angry or fearful is the patient aware of any odor; do sounds or noises distract the patient particularly during sexual activity; is music important to the patient and what kinds; does it release tension; does the patient like his partner's voice; is music ever a part of sexual activity; describe.

Principles of Interviewing. During the history-taking it is crucial that the therapist show no embarrassment, no surprise, and no prejudice in response to the patient's description of his sexual attitudes and practices.

Another Foundation principle is that the therapist approach the patient without assuming that the sexual dysfunction is caused by some personality problem. If the patient suspects that the therapist cannot accept him without labeling him neurotic, important basic information will be masked. It is a mistake to regard sexual dysfunction only as a symptom of psychiatric illness; the sexual dysfunction frequently is itself the disorder—

a disorder caused by ignorance, by emotional deprivation, by cultural pressures, by the complete removal of sex from its natural context.

Masters and Johnson emphasize that the greatest single error in taking a sex history is to regard it as having a meaning apart from the individual's history as a whole person. More important than exact accounts of the patient's problem are histories which bring out significant feelings and events revealing the marriage relationship and the attitudes of the partners. What may be traumatic to one individual may be trivial in the context of another's whole life. A relevant sex history develops material that brings out a person's attitudes, values, feelings, and expectations. To understand the aura of a person's childhood, home life, and adolescence is to understand his sexual attitudes as well. Of course, it is important to discover and to explore traumatic or variant events such as incest, illegitimate pregnancy, abortion, homosexuality, rape, and infidelity; however, emphasis is placed on understanding the whole person. "In theory," says Mrs. Johnson, "the cotherapists need only a chronological history. But this doesn't work in reality. When there are real dissensions between the two people or real past trauma, then if the cotherapists don't know a great deal more about the people involved and their own expectations than a chronology can give, the therapy program is in trouble."

Developing an accurate idea of the patient's philosophy and life style is also necessary because changes in the patient's behavior, if they are to be permanent, must fit in with his own way of living. Mrs. Johnson explains this: "It's their life that's being dealt with, their rules, their values. What we sift through and replace are those patterns of behavior, those bits of information they have that are fallacious, or are myths or superstitions, or just plain unworkable. We're on very safe ground when we do that. If a patient gives us account after account of how he clashes with his partner, then after the first history-taking sessions we feed this material back. We 'mirror' back his own material and let him be confronted by it. So really, we tell him what he's already told us."

The sex history form which appears in *Human Sexual Inadequacy* is the first one in print, and the questions in this chapter are only a sampling from that form. Masters and Johnson themselves had never written out sex history questions before they undertook preparation of their second book. They had always obtained histories without a formal list by proceeding with each patient individually in a nonrigid, nonstructured fashion following the patient's significant answers, inflections, and mannerisms wherever they led. Cotherapists Schumacher and Spitz learned the technique by observing Masters and Johnson, rather than by memorizing a formal set of questions.

Day Two

On Day Two the patients return to the Foundation for the second history-taking session. Hopefully, they have had a chance to relax and to think over the previous day's session. In the meantime, the cotherapists have reviewed the first interviews and have decided which areas need to be explored further.

With the female cotherapist now interviewing the husband, and the male cotherapist interviewing the wife, a special effort is made during this second session to discuss sensitive areas. Based on the previous interview with each patient, the cotherapists now have some clues about what parts of the history may have been left out or presented in a biased manner. The second interview is deliberately structured around these significant possibilities. It often happens that patients will give the therapist of the opposite sex information that they will not give to the therapist of the same sex. When this happens, the second day's interviews can be extremely revealing.

Do patients always tell the truth about themselves? Because the husband and wife each know that the other is being questioned along the same lines, the stories they have told are usually pretty straight. If the husband and wife, however, have previously agreed together to hold something back, the cotherapists may not realize it during the Day One and Day Two interviews. Eventually, something tips them off—a contradiction in the stories or the patient's apparent anxiety while trying to avoid that subject. A strong signal that pertinent material has been withheld is failure of the couple to progress in therapy.

Masters and Johnson say it is fairly routine that a person might have something he does not want to say in the beginning, but it generally comes out sometime during the treatment program. Even though a patient may hold back information, or lie at first, he comes to realize, from the nonjudgmental atmosphere of the sessions, that it doesn't matter. He can go ahead and tell the truth any time he feels secure enough, and no one will disapprove of him because he lied. In speaking of couples in therapy, Mrs. Johnson says, "Many marital partners enter therapy with the idea that they're going to remain in command of their own information; it's a safety-first measure. I think the majority, once they realize what the atmosphere is, change their minds." But Dr. Masters has instilled in the therapists at the Foundation a healthy respect for the individual who has decided he really wants to withhold information from his partner. Masters offers an example: "Suppose a man has some homosexual experiences in his background and prefers not to tell his wife. This husband may know that to his wife it will mean that he is incapable of marriage and she might react by leaving him eventually. By telling a marriage partner this information, the cotherapists would be taking a chance with the marriage relationship." Mrs. Johnson adds, "Once the therapists disclose this kind of information, both patients must live with it, and if it would be so devastating to their expectations that they could not deal with it, it is probably best left unsaid."

Foundation therapists do not discuss at any time anything one partner has never told the other unless permission is granted by the first partner. If the cotherapists believe it is necessary for treatment that both partners know about instances of incest, rape, homosexuality, abortion, or whatever, they discuss the situation in detail with the person involved. If the patient feels it is intolerable to share this information with the other partner or simply disagrees that it should be shared, those feelings are respected. The therapists, however, must then decide if treatment can be continued. To a great extent success in the rapid-treatment program depends on the partners' willingness to be emotionally accessible to each other, to become emotionally vulnerable to each other. It may not be in the best interest of the patients to continue the two-week therapy program if certain information cannot be shared. If such an impasse is reached, a reasonable explanation is made to the other partner, and the couple is returned to the referral source.

On the second day the therapists usually concentrate on the motivation of the patients for coming to therapy. It is important to find out if either partner was forced by the other to come for treatment. The answers to questions about what the husband and wife expect from treatment, how interested each feels the other is in the marriage and what each expects from the other, provide tremendous insight into the marriage relationship when given privately by each partner. Whether the patients regard their problem as being emotional, physical, or related to their marriage or their value systems means a great deal. The second history-taking session also gives the cotherapists a chance to cover areas they had forgotten or did not have time for on Day One.

The first two days at the Foundation are a time planned to create a relaxed and pleasant atmosphere in which it will be possible to nurture the "giving" attitudes so necessary for successful treatment. Some anxiety occurs in connection with the history-taking, but there is also the relief of being able to tell it all and of having an intelligent and highly perceptive listener. Foundation personnel are all tuned-in to making the patients feel comfortable. Especially during the first two days, when the patients' schedules are relatively light, help of the staff in providing information about vacation activities in the city is an important contribution to the program. Everything about the Foundation offices is soothing. Walls, rugs, desks and furnishings are harmoniously blended in a quiet and comfortable contemporary look. Recently, a reception center has been set up at the first floor of the building where all patients report, so that the sex therapy patients cannot be differentiated from other patients. At the Foundation offices on the second floor, there is enough room for three therapy teams to see patients, and a large conference room and library.

Day Three

On the third day of the program a medical history, physical examination, and diagnostic laboratory tests are done. Any abnormality is investigated thoroughly. Masters and Johnson emphasize that there is no excuse for treating a physical problem with psychotherapy. In their book they explain in detail for physicians which tests are used and what parts of the physical examination are especially important.

The Roundtable Discussion. After the physical examination and diagnostic tests are completed, the patients and cotherapists meet again in a session known as "the roundtable." The cotherapists have spent about seven hours in history-taking, two hours on Day One and about an hour and a half on Day Two with each patient. At this point, they are prepared to sum up and to discuss with the patients for about an hour and a half significant findings from the history-taking sessions and the physical examination. The cotherapists invite the patients—in fact, they direct them—to interrupt whenever there is an error, a misunderstanding, or any cloudiness whatever in the presentation. This direction remains in force throughout the two-week treatment period and is repeated to the patients many times. The history is never considered complete; it is thought of as an unfolding story, always open to reinterpretation or clarification. Furthermore, the patients are encouraged to disagree with the therapists whenever they feel it is necessary. As Masters and Johnson put it, "The marital partners must continue while in therapy to represent positively their own social and sexual value systems and their preferences in life-style."[1] The patients must be able to follow directions, but they must not be permitted to become subservient and unquestioning in their relationship with the cotherapists.

At the roundtable discussion the cotherapists present to the patients a probable explanation of the causes of their problem. The myths, the misinformation, the unrealistic expectations, communication failures, and destructive behavior patterns are all held up before the patients at this time so that they can get a clear and unprejudiced look at the components of their problem. Not only does it help the patients to see themselves more objectively than before, but it also helps them to be able to communicate with each other and the cotherapists. Control, confidence, and security in facing the problem take the place of arguing and defending, or silence.

At the roundtable, the cotherapists emphasize to the patients that neither of them is considered "the patient" even if one is obviously dysfunctional and the other is not. The fact that the *relationship* between the partners is the patient, and the reasons for it, are stressed again. It is especially difficult for patients who have participated in the usual one-to-one psychotherapy situation to accept this, but Masters and Johnson feel that it is crucial to success of the therapy to avoid special relationships between patient and therapist. The roundtable is not an ego-building device for any one person; it is set up to be a four-way dialogue. Only one non-

---

[1] *HSI*, p. 68.

marital alignment is allowed—the alignment between the patient and therapist of the same sex when they are attempting to explain something not understood by the other sex (the "friend in court" principle). Even so, both partners are made to understand that neither is entitled to more attention than the other from either cotherapist.

Another problem taken up at the roundtable discussion is that of "the spectator role." Dysfunctional people have become so fearful of their own performance that they mentally watch themselves and their reactions during sexual activity instead of simply allowing their natural sexual feelings to take over. When this behavior and its effect of blocking sexual stimulation is pointed out to the patients, they begin, usually for the first time in their marriage, to express to each other their worries and their fears about sexual performance.

While defining the patients' problems to them and explaining their causes, the cotherapists also explain sets of values and attitudes which may influence the patients' sexual functioning. These values and attitudes differ for everyone, and they must be taken into consideration. How these values and attitudes interact with a person's biologic capacity to function sexually is explained in the first section of Chapter 13.

The roundtable discussion may become an emotionally overwhelming experience for either partner. If this happens, the husband and wife are urged to go ahead with their discussions in private. The specific physical directions usually scheduled for Day Three are then postponed until Day Four, after the patients have had another day to talk over, think about, and adjust to the experience of the discussion and the new information they have acquired. Such intense experiences are unusual, however. Masters and Johnson say that the usual response is one of "interested participation and relief." Most frequently, patients are ready for physical direction on Day Three.

Sensate Focus. The "sensate focus" is a concept introduced eleven years ago by Masters and Johnson at the beginning of their therapy program. In recent years the idea has been popularized and in some instances bastardized, by various encounter and sensitivity groups. Basic to the sensate focus is the recognition that touch is a vital part of the personal human communication that gives meaning to sexual responsiveness for both men and women. People must touch each other in a communicative way to achieve the fullness of sexual expression. Tenderness, affection, solace, understanding, desire, warmth, comfort—almost any feeling can be conveyed to the partner by touching. When partners have lost or have never experienced the sensual pleasure of communicating by touching, the most important source of sexual stimulation is lost to them. Psychologically speaking, everyone's awareness of his own sexual responsiveness is based on his memory of the pleasure that came from sensory experiences, usually touching. The cotherapists explain that appreciation of the sense of touch is most closely related to sexual response. Touching is the way most people express and receive sexual stimuli, so that keen awareness of this sense is extremely important.

Regardless of the couple's particular sexual problem, instructions are given to them, usually at the roundtable, to choose two periods of time between the end of the roundtable on Day Three and the therapy session on Day Four during which they will explore sensory experiences, especially touch, with each other. These times are not to be chosen by the clock (unless both partners want it that way), but rather the therapists explain that they should happen naturally from the partners' shared sense of especial warmth, closeness, or even "gamesmanship." Times of tiredness, stress, or tension should be avoided. These sessions take place with no one else present in the couple's room or apartment. The partners are told to take off all their clothes first before carrying out any of the other instructions. This is to avoid distracting awkwardness or embarrassment during their time together. Of course, certain kinds of clothing, worn in a sexy way, can be stimulating, but at first it is better to avoid the risk of distraction or misunderstanding.

One partner (either one) is chosen by the cotherapists to begin giving the experience of pleasurable touching to the other. This choosing takes the burden of decision off the partners about who should begin. That partner is instructed to "trace, massage, or fondle" the other, using information from the discussion as well as both verbal and nonverbal directions from the "getting" partner about preferences for locations and intensity of touching. The idea is for the "giving" partner to provide pleasure and to discover what touching experiences are most pleasurable for the "getting" partner. The only responsibility of the person being touched is to keep the other from doing anything unpleasant, distracting, or irritating. It is not necessary to say that something feels good unless the expression is spontaneous. Neither does the "getting" partner need to feel a "rush to return the favor." At this time, touching of the genitals of either person or touching the woman's breasts is prohibited; specific sexual stimulation is forbidden.

For many people, these times are the first they have had in their lives to "think and feel sensuously" without any kind of pressure to proceed to intercourse. Another point emphasized by Masters and Johnson is that they do not structure the sensate focus exercises for the patients. They try to avoid telling the patients specifically what to do at this stage in therapy. The patients get hints from the history-taking and the discussion, but they are left to work out the details of sensate focus themselves so that the experience becomes *theirs* and not something set up for them.

The "giving" partner, in addition to providing pleasure, is directed to explore at the same time his own pleasure in touching the "getting" partner. He is expected, as Masters and Johnson put it, "to experience and appreciate the sensuous dimensions of hard and soft, smooth and rough, warm and cool, qualities of texture and, finally, the somewhat indescribable aura of physical receptivity expressed by the partner being pleasured."[2] Whenever the partners feel so inclined, they are to change roles and repeat the experience. The first try at sensate activity may seem awkward and artificial, but most people quickly catch on and begin to feel mutual pleasure and a new closeness.

Day Four

The therapy session on Day Four usually begins with a discussion of the actions and reactions of the husband and wife in following the instructions given at the previous day's sessions. At least part of the therapy sessions every day are discussions of how successful or unsuccessful the partners have been in discovering what is physically pleasing to the other. Many husbands and

[2] *HSI*, p. 73.

wives are delighted at the results of their first try at sensate focus. For the first time, they have been able to give and receive pleasure without feeling pressured toward a goal. Their success gives them a feeling of warmth and closeness, which is excellent motivation to proceed in therapy. Other couples are not successful during the first "pleasuring" trial. Anger, rejection, or even previously unknown emotional problems may come to the surface. The therapists have to be aware of all the possibilities and be able to deal with these problems as they present themselves.

On Day Four, after discussion of the couple's first attempts at sensate focus, they are instructed to try sensate exploration two more times before the next therapy session on Day Five. Again they choose two convenient periods of time, and again they take turns as the "giving" and "getting" partner. The repetition of "pleasuring" takes place on every subsequent day of the treatment program. Repetition insures that this element of expression by touching becomes a part of the couple's own way of interaction.

The Day Four "pleasuring" sessions are different from those on Day Three, however, because the therapists have added two more instructions to be followed. The first is that the person who is receiving the "pleasuring" must participate actively by putting his or her hand over the hand of the "giving" partner to show personal preference by light pressure or change of direction. *One of the most destructive myths in our culture is that men automatically know all there is to know about sex and that they can divine women's sexual needs.* Of course, this is impossible. Many women themselves do not know what stimulates them most. Knowing about sex is also supposed to be the sole responsibility of men. Actually, a spontaneous sexual interaction with both partners free to express themselves is the most stimulating situation possible, but in this case, signal systems lead each partner to the specific stimulation desired by the other. Development of these signal systems is what the therapists are after in getting the partners to express their needs to each other by touching.

The other instruction added by the therapists on Day Four is that touch should be extended to include the genitals and the wife's breasts. This, however, is to be done in a manner which in no way demands a sexual response from the partner. The therapists instruct the couple to make no effort to cause ejaculation or orgasm.

During the talk session on Day Four, the cotherapists also make sure that both husband and wife understand the anatomy of the genital organs. Since the male's genitals are external and visible, there usually is no misunderstanding about them. It is surprising, however, how many husbands have never seen the wife's genitals and have very little idea of female anatomy. Charts and models are used to explain all anatomic relationships to the couple, and the wife is encouraged to let her husband look at her genitals if he has never done so previously.

Sexual tensions which develop spontaneously during the senate focus exercises are the "ultimate purpose," but cotherapists ask the patients about their responses in a way that does not imply failure if there has been no sexual response. Rather, the questioning is used to show the patients how response develops naturally from touching, feeling, and communicating.

Mistakes. "Patients come to St. Louis to make their mistakes," says Mrs. Johnson. She explains that the cotherapists do not want the patients to report perfect and completely successful experiences in response to their instructions. They want the partners to make mistakes as they become involved sexually. If mistakes are explained in relation to the couple's own experience, they will learn much more than they would if allowed to present a perfect record. Mistakes are explained in a nonjudgmental way, and the fallacies, superstitions, or myths which led to the errors are aired too. It is important for the therapists to deal with these errors daily so that there will be no performance fears built up around them.

If the patients do not make mistakes, the cotherapists arrange a situation during the treatment program in which they will. Masters tells the story of a patient with premature ejaculation who bragged that he had the control technique mastered in a session or two. The patient was learning control in the female superior position, which is the best one for this purpose. Masters, knowing from the history that the patient would revert to his customary man-on-top position if left to himself, said, "Okay, go ahead on your own!" Sure enough, the patient tried to have intercourse that night in the male superior position, the most difficult for ejaculatory control. He ejaculated prematurely—but subsequently he was willing to listen closely to instructions and allow the cotherapists to set the pace during the rest of the therapy sessions.

Special Use of Lotions. Roughness and dryness of some patients' hands presented a problem at the beginning of the treatment program. This led to extensive experiments with lotions at the Foundation. Several important observations came out of these studies. First, some patients who could never touch their partners' genitals were able to do so by applying lotions. Being directed to apply a pleasant familiar medium to the partner's body gave the spouse "permission" to touch anywhere while applying it. In addition, some people who reacted negatively to body fluids—seminal fluid and vaginal lubrication—overcame this while using the lotion during sensate focus exercises. Third, Masters and Johnson have noted a striking correlation between objection to the use of lotions and treatment failure. The patients who felt that use of the lotion was unaccepable had a failure rate more than four times as great as the overall failure rate for the program. Although it is too soon to say for sure, Masters and Johnson suggest that a negative attitude toward using lotions in "pleasuring" the partner may be a strong indication that difficult or complex problems are present.

Continuing the Treatment Program. On Day Five, after two days of sensate focus opportunities, the therapists and patients embark upon treatment of the specific problem which brought the couple to the Foundation. The most common sexual problems are premature ejaculation, impotence, orgasmic dysfunction, painful intercourse, and problems relating to aging. Much less frequent are ejaculatory incompetence and vaginismus. During the treatment program the couple will spend between twelve and thirty hours with the therapists in addition to their "homework." Dr. Masters comments, "Results show quickly. Even the patients notice it. When they are in their second week here they comment to the staff that they can always tell if the patients sitting in the waiting room are in the first week of therapy from the look on their faces. After the first week the difference in faces is phenomenal. They look better and so much more at ease. It doesn't take too many days before you can observe a couple walking down the street holding hands and looking as if they are beginning to enjoy each other."

CHAPTER 9

Premature Ejaculation

Most men who have premature ejaculation give the same history. All their early heterosexual attempts were hurried. A prostitute may have congratulated her client on his speedy performance because it meant she could go on to the next customer. A young man having intercourse in the back seat of a car at a lovers' lane may have been worried about being caught in the act. Emphasis on speedy ejaculation as a desirable accomplishment can easily become a way of life after only a few such episodes. Once this rapid ejaculating pattern is imprinted, it frequently is there to stay. Masters and Johnson say that this kind of early training is the most prominent cause of premature ejaculation in adults.

They define premature ejaculation as inability to delay ejaculation long enough for the woman to have orgasm fifty percent of the time. If the female is not able to have orgasm for reasons other than the rapid ejaculation of her partner, this definition does not apply. Other therapists define premature ejaculation as inability to delay ejaculating for thirty seconds to a minute after the penis is in the vagina. The Foundation's definition takes emphasis away from a time period and considers the satisfaction of both partners as the primary criterion. In any case, premature ejaculation is the most common sexual dysfunction of men, and Masters and Johnson estimate that millions of men and their wives are affected by it.

One of the great difficulties with this pattern of sex release is that it places no value on sexual satisfaction for the female; it is oriented only to the man's pleasure. The point is made again and again throughout *Human Sexual Inadequacy* that one must "give" to "get." Many men who ejaculate without satisfying their partners think that sexual pleasure is a male prerogative. They are unaware that sexual pleasure derived from giving brings enormous benefits to the total relationship.

Human Sexual Inadequacy reveals a direct correlation between a man's educational level and his concern about satisfying his wife. High-school dropouts rarely complain about premature ejaculation, although their wives may. Many of these men regard their wives as sexual receptacles who are not supposed to have or to express sexual feelings of their own. Men whose educational level is higher, and whose sophistication is greater, are more likely to feel that their masculinity is threatened by failure to satisfy their wives.

When a man consistently ejaculates prematurely, the pattern of his marriage is somewhat predictable. At first, when the newlyweds discover that the husband cannot delay his ejaculation, they lovingly console each other and assure themselves that the situation will improve after they become accustomed to married life. Eventually many men do gain control, but millions do not.

When the problem persists, the wife's attitude begins to change. She starts to feel that she is being inconsiderately used, that her husband is concerned only with his own pleasure and that he has no appreciation of her sexual needs. At every sexual encounter, her husband ejaculates so quickly before or just after entering that she has no opportunity to reach a climax. Especially after stimulating foreplay, the wife is left with no means of release and a lot of resentment.

A man with premature ejaculation tries endless psychologic and physical devices to break the pattern. Mental distractions such as counting backward from one hundred, thinking of a business problem, or recalling a vacation trip are the usual initial stratagems. When these techniques fail, a man will resort to concentrating on contracting his anal sphincter, pinching himself, or pulling his hair. Frequently various creams and lotions are applied to anesthetize the penis to prevent ejaculation. Some men can delay ejaculation for a short time by employing these devices. However, the total result is unsatisfying because the distraction keeps the man from losing himself fully in the sexual experience. He cannot enjoy intercourse in an uninhibited, passionate way. His partner becomes aware of his distance and restraint, and her pleasure is diminished.

In the usual course of events, after a period of years, husband and wife both withdraw from some of the commitment of marriage, the man doubting his masculinity and the wife losing her confidence in herself as a woman. As the man becomes more and more humiliated over his failure to satisfy his wife, he may even lose his ability to have an erection. A quiet but hostile marriage without sex may endure, but many end in divorce.

Many men with premature ejaculation seem incapable of thinking of a wife's needs. Masters and Johnson have found that most of these men are selfish and do not consider themselves inadequate lovers. Many blame their wives for not being sexy enough. It never occurs to them that *they* are inadequate. Actually, these men, especially older ones, can hardly be blamed; the idea that women are entitled to sexual pleasure is a relatively recent one in our culture.

One of the most important chapters in *Human Sexual Inadequacy* is the one on premature ejaculation. Anyone concerned with this problem should read Masters and Johnson's original text with care; they present in detail for the first time their highly effective technique for learning ejaculatory control. The significance of this one treatment technique is almost immeasurable. Millions of men with the problem of premature ejaculation can learn how to satisfy their wives, improve their own sex lives, and avoid the marital difficulties related in the preceding pages. This technique, however, is not a do-it-yourself panacea. Many men who ejaculate prematurely do not communicate with their wives and would, in fact, need a therapist to get communication going between them before they could appreciate that there was a problem. Probably many of these men will not even try the Masters and Johnson method because they are neither willing to admit they have a problem nor willing to take the emotional risk of trying to solve it.

Wives of men with premature ejaculation usually initiate treatment, often after many years of marriage when their children are grown. During the childbearing years, women's psychic and physical energies usually are diverted by the needs of their families. Later they may feel that they are missing out. Then they often seek help and insist that their husbands seek help. Sometimes they try extramarital affairs—heterosexual, homosexual, or both.

Treatment

The first step in treatment at the Foundation is to assure the couple that the pattern of premature ejaculation can be reversed. Confidence in themselves is important. The wife must appreciate that the husband may be afraid the treatment will not work and approach him with understanding.

Usually, when premature ejaculation is a problem, the couple has adopted the technique of not touching the man's genitals. Sometimes their physician or another sex counselor is responsible for advising them to do this. Not only is the avoidance technique a failure, but it also deprives the woman of the pleasure of wanton touching and the man the pleasure of being fondled. Masters and Johnson use a "touching" technique which brings the man control and brings the couple the freedom of caressing each other without ever having to think "Don't touch."[1]

In the first few days of therapy the husband and wife have practiced "pleasuring" each other during the sensate focus sessions. (See Chapter 8.) On the fifth or sixth day of therapy the cotherapists explain to the couple how to begin specific training for ejaculatory control during their next "homework" sessions. The woman is instructed to sit on the bed, leaning comfortably on a pillow and supported by the headboard. The man, lying on his back, facing her, positions his body between her legs, with his feet placed on the mattress on the outside of her thighs as shown in Fig. 4. Masters

---

[1] The direct genital approach was first introduced by James H. Semans in "Premature Ejaculation: A New Approach," *Southern Medical Journal*, 49 (1956), pp. 353-357.

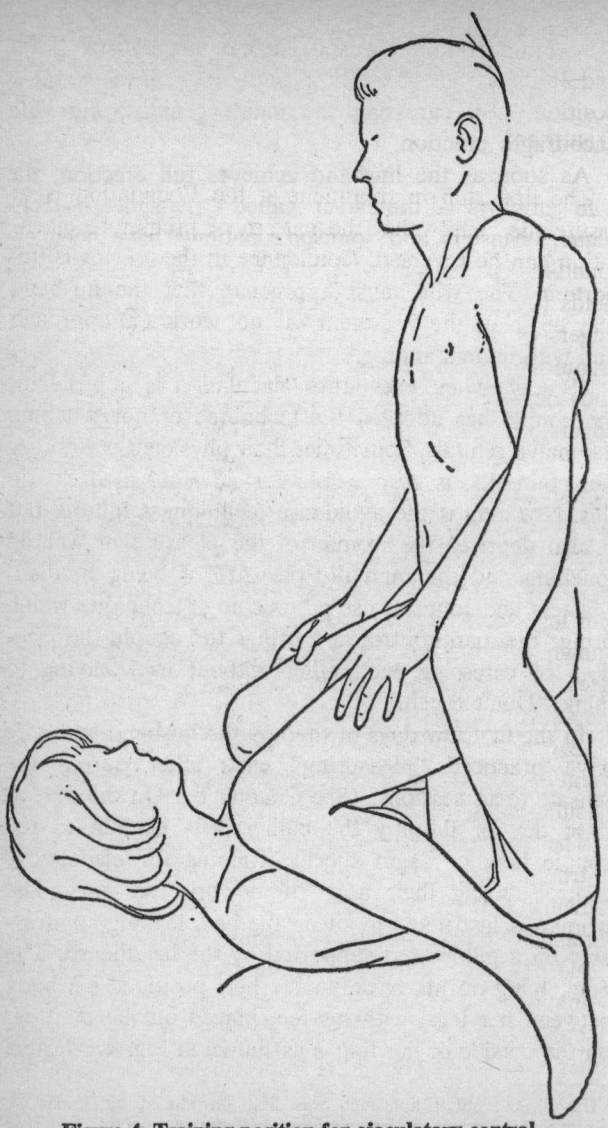

Figure 4. Training position for ejaculatory control.

and Johnson call this the "ejaculatory control training position." By caressing the man's genitals, the wife encourages erection.

As soon as the husband achieves full erection, the wife employs a maneuver called "the squeeze technique." Masters and Johnson's patients have been astoundingly successful with this technique. The woman holds the penis between her thumb and the first two fingers of the same hand. The thumb is placed on the frenulum (the underside of the penis, just where the shaft ends and the head of the penis begins), and the two fingers are placed on the opposite side from the thumb, one on each side of the ridge which separates the glans from the shaft. The woman then squeezes her thumb and first two fingers together with a fairly hard pressure for three or four seconds. The pressure makes the man lose his urge to ejaculate and may also make him lose some of his erection; why this happens is not known. After fifteen to thirty seconds, the wife manipulates her partner to full erection once more and uses the squeeze technique again to prevent ejaculation. By repeating this procedure it is easy to have fifteen to twenty minutes of continuous sex play and no ejaculation.

The therapists must make certain that the wife is instructed correctly in placing her fingers. They use drawings and artificial models to be sure the couple understands the anatomic relationships. The squeeze technique may be used three or four times during the first training session. This play is not planned to lead to ejaculation, only to accustom the male to the squeeze experience. Even fairly hard squeezing does not hurt the erect penis.

The quick effectiveness of this therapy gives the

couple new confidence immediately and opens physical and verbal communication channels that previously have been blocked. It usually takes only two or three days after the first training session on Day Five or Six of the treatment program for a couple to learn ejaculatory control. For people who have never had the problem of premature ejaculation, it is difficult to appreciate the happiness this accomplishment brings to both husband and wife.

The next step for the partners, after they have learned some control, is to have the penis inserted in the vagina, but without thrusting. The man lies flat on his back, and the woman straddles him in the superior coital position as shown in Figure 5. After the squeeze technique has been applied two or three times the wife inserts the penis into her vagina. She remains motionless so that her husband gets used to the new feeling of penile containment without any immediate urge to ejaculate. Before therapy the usual pattern for couples who have the premature ejaculation problem is for the husband to stimulate the wife almost to orgasm and then to enter. The wildly excited woman would thrust frantically in an effort to reach orgasm before the man ejaculated, but her excitement would only have the effect of bringing the man to orgasm immediately. With this technique, the wife's restraint gives the man a chance to achieve control.

If the man feels he is going to ejaculate, the woman merely raises her body and repeats the squeeze procedure, then shortly after reinserts the penis.

After a few days' practice with the squeeze technique, the husband is instructed to thrust just enough to maintain his erection. The husband and wife find they can stay in the female superior coital position for fifteen to twenty minutes before ejaculation. Bringing about their

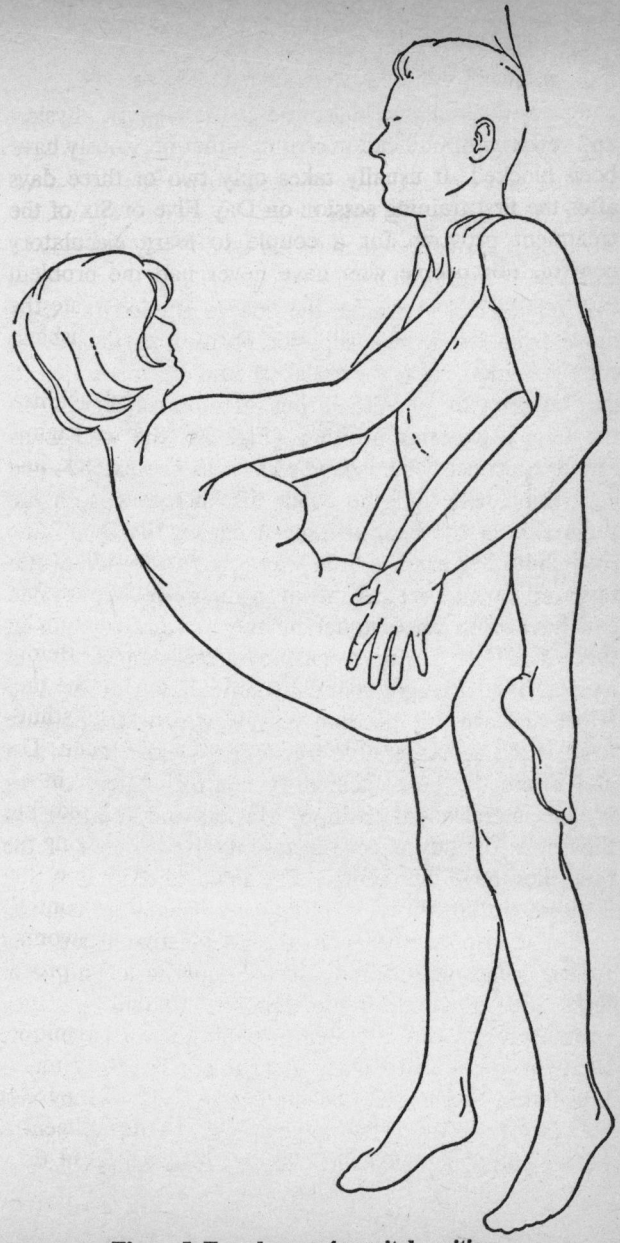

Figure 5. Female superior coital position.

own cure gives the partners enormous confidence. The wife, frequently for the first time, has the opportunity to think and feel sexually. Many such women who have never had orgasm because their husbands ejaculated too quickly now find themselves completely responsive and able to reach climax.

After control increases, the couple is encouraged to move from the female superior position to the lateral coital position. A few 'trials" should be made before they attempt to convert during intercourse. Starting in the female superior position (Fig. 5), the wife leans forward against her husband's chest as she extends one leg behind her, while he bends his knee that is on the same side of the bed, keeping it flat on the sheet. She then slides her trunk a little way toward the side of her husband's bent knee, as shown in Figure 6. The woman can have both knees touching the bed for traction in thrusting. Both partners can move freely and both can have a hand free for manual manipulation. The small effort to learn this position is well worthwhile because it gives the most possible freedom for experimentation and offers the best ejaculatory control. After couples try the lateral coital position, Masters and Johnson say they subsequently choose it seventy-five percent of the time they have intercourse. The male superior position is the most difficult in which to gain ejaculatory control.

The therapists explain to the couple that when they return home they should use the squeeze technique at least once a week for the first six months, and they should practice it for fifteen or twenty minutes at some time during the wife's menstrual period. They are told to proceed in other sexual encounters in their own natural way of lovemaking. It usually takes six to twelve months before complete ejaculatory control is accomplished.

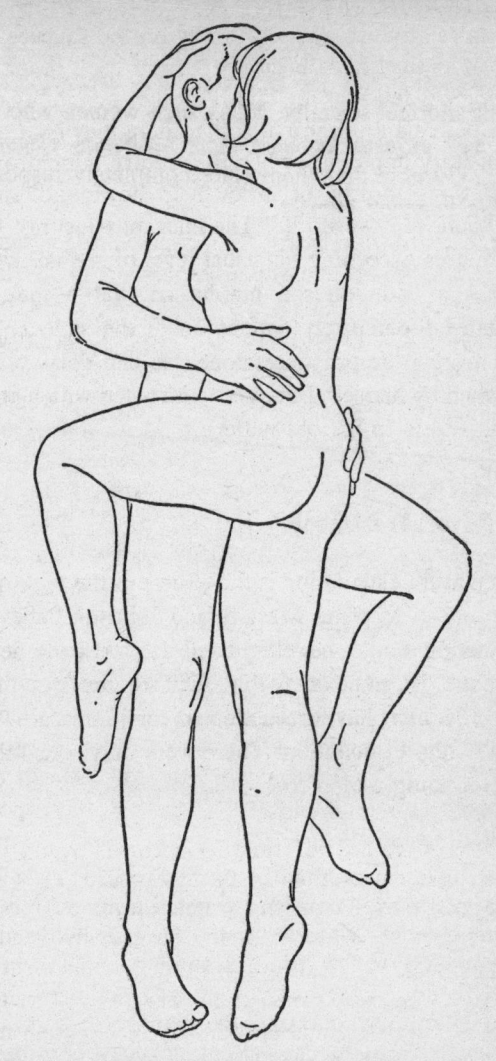

Figure 6. Lateral coital position.

Couples are also advised to rely on the squeeze technique after they have been apart from each other for a time and sex tensions are high. Another possibility about which patients are warned, is that there may be a period of transitory impotence when they return home from the Foundation, mostly because their newfound success leads them to "overdo it." The man may just not be up to demands exceeding his usual level of sexual activity.

Masters and Johnson emphasize that a man who ejaculates prematurely cannot make the squeeze technique work if he practices alone. He can delay ejaculation when by himself, but once confronted with a partner he will revert to his old pattern.

Results of Treatment

Premature ejaculation is the easiest of the male sexual inadequacies to treat. Masters and Johnson believe this dysfunction could be eliminated in a decade if their technique is made available. During the past eleven years 186 men have been treated for premature ejaculation at the Foundation. There were only four failures, an astounding rate of success!

> As more sex information becomes available, as more acceptance of a single standard of sexual expression for man and woman develops in our culture, the sense of shared responsibility for female sexual release is assuming equal stature with, and presumably soon will supplant, the time-honored concept of the woman's subservient role in her mate's sexual gratification. With both a sense of responsibility and sufficient knowledge

of effective sexual function must come major sociological improvement in the male capacity for ejaculatory control.[2]

---

[2] *HSI*, p. 101.

CHAPTER 10

Ejaculatory Incompetence

Because ejaculatory incompetence is relatively rare, many doctors and marriage counselors do not even know what it is, and the general public knows nothing at all about it. Ejaculatory incompetence is the opposite of premature ejaculation. The term refers to the inability to ejaculate in the vagina. A man who has premature ejaculation cannot delay ejaculating once his penis is inserted, or sometimes he ejaculates even before entry. The man with ejaculatory incompetence is able to have and maintain an erection and keep his penis in the vagina for thirty minutes to an hour, but he has a mental block against allowing his seminal fluid to enter the vagina. Because these men can maintain an erection for such long periods, their wives frequently have more than one orgasm.

Most of these men can masturbate or easily be manipulated to orgasm by another person. Some of them can have orgasm during fellatio. It is when the penis is in the vagina that they fail. Only three of the seventeen men treated at the Foundation for this condition had never been able to ejaculate at all, regardless of the form of stimulation.

Many factors can contribute to this condition, some of which are religious restrictions, fear of impregnating, and lack of physical interest or active dislike for the female partner.

For example, one especially religious young Jewish man, whose usual behavior was shy, retiring, and unaggressive, unexpectedly and unaccountably forced himself upon a young woman, only to have her plead with him at the last minute to stop because she was menstruating. Horrified at his own behavior, the young man fled immediately. Firm restrictions are placed upon orthodox Jews against having intercourse during menstruation and for several days following. Only after this specified time is the vagina considered clean and acceptable for entry. When this young man married several years later, he retained such strong feelings about the vagina as an unclean area that he was not able to ejaculate during intercourse.

There are instances, Master and Johnson report, when husbands dislike their wives so intensely that they take pleasure in holding back to frustrate them. One man who married for money and social position just could not get excited enough about his wife to ejaculate intravaginally with her, although he maintained relationships with other women with whom it was easy for him to perform.

Other men are so afraid of getting their wives pregnant that the fear, which can be conscious or unconscious, makes them unable to ejaculate.

A single particularly traumatic event can condition a man to withhold his ejaculate. Four of the seventeen men referred to the Foundation for ejaculatory incompetence had been able to ejaculate intravaginally with their wives until a traumatic event blocked their response. Masters and Johnson tell the story of a man who, returning home unexpectedly, found his wife having intercourse with another man. The wife's lover had just ejaculated as the husband walked into the bedroom. The husband's first view of the scene was the other man's semen seeping from his wife's vagina. The husband and wife remained married, but the man was not able to ejaculate intravaginally again. He felt that his wife's vagina was contaminated by the other man's semen. The thought of letting his own semen mix with the other man's was so repugnant that he could not ejaculate.

Masters and Johnson have treated men who were caught masturbating as youngsters and were so severely punished by their parents that they were not able to ejaculate in later life. Others experienced such strong parental disapproval as teenagers for having wet dreams that they found it impossible, years later after marriage, to experience orgasm during intercourse.

Treatment

Both ejaculatory incompetence and premature ejaculation can lead to secondary impotence. This is especially true when a man's sexual competence is under attack by a sexually demanding female over a period of time. If impotence does develop, Masters and Johnson concentrate on treating the impotence first and then the problem of ejaculatory incompetence or premature ejaculation.

The treatment approach to the man who cannot ejaculate begins with the sensate focus "pleasuring" techniques on Day Three or Four of the treatment program. On Day Five or Six or whenever the cotherapists feel the husband and wife are ready to proceed, they instruct the wife to stimulate her husband in whatever ways he finds most exciting. After he is sufficiently aroused, she manipulates the penis in as stimulating a manner as possible. The idea is for her to cause ejaculation so that he will identify this pleasure with her rather than regarding her as a threat. Her efforts should not be rushed; it may be necessary to repeat the technique over several days before it is successful. Once ejaculation happens in the presence of the woman, and as a result of her activity, both appreciate the experience as a pleasurable one that they have shared.

Many wives, because they have been frustrated for years by an incomprehensible situation are at first unwilling to cooperate in giving their husbands pleasure and release through the masturbatory exercise. The wife's initial reaction may be that she is the one who has been denied. She may feel that the treatment should be oriented to her sexual satisfaction. In this situation, the importance of the dual-sex team is especially apparent. The advice and instructions offered by male and female therapists to a husband and wife are far more forceful than similar advice and instructions coming from a therapist of either sex to only one of the marital partners. Imagine a sexually incompetent man, involved in a shaky marriage, who comes home from a therapy session and tells his wife to manipulate him to orgasm. Once the therapy team is able to convince the wife that she must "give" to "get," instructions usually are followed, and the treatment is more likely to work. Husbands are also advised to give their wives sexual release during the time of these exercises because their sexual tensions are bound to rise.

After the masturbation technique has succeeded, and

ejaculation can be accomplished easily with it, the next step is to have the female insert the penis after having manually aroused her mate to a point near ejaculation. The wife should be in the female superior position (Fig. 5), sitting over the man who is lying on his back, and kneeling with her knees outside his thighs. She is instructed, once his penis is inserted, to move demandingly until ejaculation occurs. If the wife even with unrestrained pelvic thrusting is unable to cause intravaginal ejaculation after a period of time, she is instructed to slip the penis out and go back to manual stimulation. After she brings the man close to ejaculation again, she reinserts his penis and tries once more.

If he ejaculates just as he enters, this is still encouraging. If he can get even a few drops of semen in the vagina, it is often enough to break the phobic pattern. Masters and Johnson have told how dramatic a moment this can be for two people who have worried about this problem perhaps for many years. The psychologic advantages that come to the couple through their new closeness are immeasurable.

After the first ejaculatory successes, the therapists instruct the husband and wife about prolonging the amount of time the penis is in the vagina before ejaculation so that the wife can have orgasm.

The important thread running through all of Masters and Johnson's therapy program is the need for communication between partners. They regard intercourse as the ultimate in communication. If couples can be brought together and feelings of love and consideration can be encouraged and expressed, a favorable climate for correcting sexual problems is created.

Results

Of the seventeen men treated for ejaculatory incompetence at the Foundation, only three were treatment failures. One of these was the orthodox Jewish man who had unknowingly tried to force his sexual attentions on a menstruating woman; another was the man who found his wife in bed just after her lover had ejaculated. The third man had absolutely no interest in his wife. In this last instance, Masters and Johnson recommended that the wife divorce her husband, but the wife was reluctant to do so.

One successfully treated man disliked his wife intensely and led a homosexual life on the side. The results of the treatment worked out to the satisfaction of both. The man learned to ejaculate intravaginally, which satisfied his wife. He continued with his homosexual activities, which satisfied him and which his wife knew about and condoned.

Three couples in addition to the seventeen other men treated by Masters and Johnson for ejaculatory incompetence made an interesting choice. Originally they had been referred to the Foundation for their fertility problem. Once they learned that the wife could become pregnant by correction of ejaculatory incompetence or by artificial insemination with the man's semen, they chose artificial insemination, preferring to use their dysfunction as a birth-control device.

CHAPTER 11

Primary and Secondary Impotence

"There has never been an impotent woman," according to Masters and Johnson. Excepting women with rare anatomic or psychosomatic abnormalities, any woman can have intercourse and produce children merely by passive acceptance of a man's sexual advances. Not so for the unfortunate male.

> The cultural concept that the male partner must accept full responsibility for establishing successful coital connection has placed upon every man the psychological burden for the coital process and has released every woman from any suggestion of similar responsibility for its success.[1]

The impotent male cannot have intercourse and cannot reproduce, either because he cannot get an erection hard enough to enter the vagina, or because he cannot maintain his erection long enough after entry to ejaculate. In their discussion of impotence, Masters and Johnson stress the need for an accurate classification of the male sexual inadequacies. Premature ejaculation, they explain, has long been classified as a form of

---
[1] *HSI*, p. 159.

impotence, but clearly it is not, because erection happens easily and ejaculation occurs immediately. The man with ejaculatory incompetence is not impotent either. He can get a hard erection and keep it for an hour or more, but cannot ejaculate in the vagina.

Confusion about the difference between impotence and sterility also abounds. A man who is sterile but not impotent can have an erection and ejaculate, but he cannot have children because he does not have enough sperm cells or because his sperm cells are defective. Although he cannot reproduce, a sterile man can function perfectly well sexually. Conversely, an impotent man may be fertile—that is he may produce live sperm cells sufficient for reproduction; however, he is not able to reproduce by having intercourse.

Ignorance about these matters is unfortunate and dramatizes the need for sex education. The opponents of teaching about sex in the public schools might consider Masters and Johnson's unqualified assertion that *it is ignorance more than anything else that causes sexual dysfunction*. Frequently those who object most strenuously to the dissemination of sex information have the most need for it.

Primary Impotence

Anxiety related to sexual activity and insecurity as a person can be incapacitating enough to overcome completely a man's natural ability to have an erection. Such a man has *never* been able to have intercourse, either vaginally or rectally, with a female partner or with a male partner. Masters and Johnson have called this condition "primary impotence." During the eleven years they have offered therapy, thirty-two primarily impotent males have been treated. Twenty-one were not married when they were in therapy, but some of them had been married previously. Frequently their marriages ended in divorce or annulment because of their sexual inadequacy. Others were married for many years without ever having intercourse. One primarily impotent man treated at the Foundation had not consummated his marriage in eighteen years.

Assignment of a single cause of primary impotence in an individual is probably incorrect. Several familial and societal influences destructive to the personality development of young boys recurred regularly in Masters and Johnson's patients. A brief discussion of these follows.

The Seductive Mother. Among the men treated for primary impotence were three instances of specific sexual overtures by mothers toward their sons. In these families the father was either absent or ineffective as a person. In each instance the son slept in the mother's bedroom at least through puberty. Though no patient gave a history of incest, some reported masturbation by their mothers and other sexual overtures.

Religious Belief in Sex as Sin. Masters and Johnson say repeatedly that the single most common factor in the backgrounds of sexually dysfunctional people is rigid adherence to religious restrictions. Six primarily impotent men from families that demanded unquestioning obedience to religious rules, two Jews and four Catholics, were in no way prepared for marriage. Taboos and misinformation doomed them to erective failure. These men chose mates with equally restrictive religious backgrounds, five of whom had an unusual and severe sexual dysfunction called "vaginismus." (See Chapter 14.)

Homosexuality. Another six of the thirty-two primarily impotent men had had homosexual attachments as teenagers, and still considered themselves basically homophile in orientation. They felt that their pleasurable and relatively long-term liaisons with men had committed them to permanent homosexual identification. Three of these six men had domineering mothers, but the others were from reasonably normal families. Although some of the families expected their sons to go to church regularly, none was fanatic about it. Two of the six had married some time after their homosexual relationship had ended. One was still with his wife at the time of treatment, but the marriage of the other had been annulled. After sexual failure in marriage, both had tried psychotherapy, but neither was able to achieve security in thinking and feeling sexually about his wife.

Masters and Johnson recorded an interesting observation of the men in this group. All six said they wanted to function sexually with women, but what is important, only two wanted to refrain permanently from homosexual relations. This desire to share both sex worlds undoubtedly contributed to the difficulty they had in participating heterosexually. They were unwilling to make the commitment to heterosexuality that would allow their sexual feelings to be channeled in one direction.

Traumatic Initial Failure. Four of the thirty-two primarily impotent men in the series had had humiliating initial sexual experiences with prostitutes. The squalid quarters, repelling physical appearance of the women and their degrading approach made sexual arousal for the young men impossible. The prostitutes' amusement and derision destroyed their self-confidence. These young men, who had unremarkable family histories, were unable to have intercourse with other women because it had become a degrading experience in their eyes, one to be avoided.

Of the remaining thirteen of the thirty-two primarily impotent men, no two offered the same story of initial sexual trauma leading to failure and impotence. Nor was there any specific family pattern, such as a strong mother and weak father.

Some patients who were not impotent had case histories indicating more severe sexual trauma than the impotent patients. Why were they not impotent? And why have other men, who failed in their initial attempt at intercourse, overcome the trauma? Masters and Johnson say there are no ready answers. Not enough is known about the susceptibility of these men to psychologic trauma or their individual personality characteristics to supply specific answers.

Secondary Impotence

A man with secondary impotence cannot maintain or perhaps even get an erection, but has succeeded at vaginal or rectal intercourse at least one time. Usually, the secondarily impotent male has a history of many successful entries before impotence occurs. The occasional failure that most men experience because of tiredness or distraction is not to be confused with secondary impotence.

Masters and Johnson classify a man as secondarily impotent if he has erective failure during at least twenty-five percent of his sexual opportunities. Among their patients the most frequent antecedents of secondary impotence were premature ejaculation and continuous and excessive use of alcohol. Other common causes were overbearing parents, religious restrictions, and homosexuality. A long or serious illness may also precede secondary impotence, as may heart attacks, even if they are mild, and prostate surgery; among these men it is more likely that the impotence is related to psychologic trauma caused by the illness rather than physical disability. Very few men develop physiologic or anatomic abnormalities that make them impotent. Masters and Johnson's clinical experience indicates that any biologic or physical factor casting doubt on a male's sexual adequacy is a threat to his ego. Once the fear of failure is present, men become highly susceptible to secondary impotence.

Premature Ejaculation. In the Masters and Johnson study, sixty-three of the 213 secondarily impotent men had a long-term pattern of ejaculating prematurely. After marriage a man with this problem gradually becomes aware of his unsatisfactory performance and his wife begins expressing openly her own sexual frustrations. As his sense of inadequacy deepens, he tries more and more desperately all the usual techniques to delay ejaculation. But instead of helping, these distractions put him in the role of an observer in his own marriage bed. This psychic "holding back" is a step toward secondary impotence. The man deliberately blocks all sexually stimulating signals from his wife. Instead of losing himself in his natural response to her caresses, her bodily movement, and her facial expression, he distracts himself from these and concentrates only on avoiding ejaculation. Over a period of time this deliberate blocking of sexual stimuli leads to an episode of erective failure.

Now aware of a even more threatening inadequacy,

the husband worries about having an erection. If he fails again, he tries to will an erection so that he can satisfy his wife's demand for fulfillment. This cannot work. The typical man in this circumstance finds excuses not to participate in sex. When his wife finally demands it, his fears of failure are so strong that he does fail. At this stage he has become secondarily impotent.

Drinking Pattern. Masters and Johnson say their typical patient who develops secondary impotence related to drinking is a successful businessman, thirty-five to fifty-five years old. They treated thirty-five men whose histories had the following pattern.

A couple of drinks at a business lunch, cocktails on arriving home, wine with dinner, and maybe a nightcap are usual. Excessive drinking at evening social events is rather frequent. After one such evening of overindulgence, the man approaches his wife for intercourse and finds he cannot get an erection. The next morning he is fuzzy about what happened the night before, but he does know that he failed sexually, and it bothers him. Later that day, brooding about it over lunch, he might have another drink or two. That evening, after heavy consumption of alcohol during the day, he attempts intercourse again. He is so concerned about failure that, of course, he fails again. With no erection for the second time, he goes into a state of panic. After this second failure, secondary impotence may be established.

At this stage his wife begins to wonder if her husband no longer cares for her, and often she will make more sexual demands than usual. This pressure to perform may be just enough to keep the man in a totally impotent state. If she appreciates her husband's difficulty and decides to avoid sex unless he wants it, he senses her concern and has additional fears of being unable to perform. She can do nothing right because of his fear. Men are extremely sensitive to such fears, say Masters and Johnson, because sexual performance is demanded from them as proof of their personal worth.

A Dominating Parent. Sexual insecurity and subsequent secondary impotence are often associated with dominance of the family by either the father or mother. In *Human Sexual Inadequacy* there are twenty-three case histories in which a disapproving, demanding parent, male or female, set impossible goals for a child, thus destroying the young male's confidence in his sexuality and masculinity.

Sons of dominant women often choose domineering wives. These women continue the mother's pattern of overwhelming their husbands until they rebel by ducking behind the curtain of secondary impotence as a way of avoiding the female onslaught. Sons of overcontrolling fathers may alternate between admiring the father and hating him. One son, whose self-confidence was completely undermined by a perfectionist father, failed at several jobs. Finally he felt forced to accept a position with his father's company in order to provide for his family. His fears of job performance in that situation were so strong, they easily transferred to his sex life. The son felt he could not match the strength or masculinity of his father, and he retreated into failure in performance at the job and in bed.

Religious Restriction. Of the 213 men treated for secondary impotence, the condition of twenty-six was directly related to their upbringing in extremely religious families where sex was regarded as degrading if not sinful. Of these, six were Jewish, eleven Catholic, four fundamentalist Protestant, and five mixed marriages. Religious prohibitions cause extreme stress when a man

UNDERSTANDING HUMAN SEXUAL INADEQUACY

first tries to have intercourse. Most men manage the event with reasonable security, but some do not. In speaking of difficulties that religious beliefs may bring to marriage Masters and Johnson comment:

> There can be no appreciation that sexual functioning is indeed a natural physical phenomenon, when material of sexual content is considered overwhelmingly embarrassing, personally degrading, and often is theologically prohibited.[2]

The troubles of couples from restrictive and controlling religious families often multiply when they recognize their sexual problem and decide to do something about it. They usually go to their clergyman for assistance. Frequently he is ill equipped to help and often tells the couple their sexual problem is not important. This leaves the unfortunate supplicants caught in a trap. Their religious counselor says they have no problem, but they know better. Each withdraws, wondering if something is wrong with him or his mate, but not communicating his concern because supposedly no problem exists. Masters and Johnson do say that a good number of people are able to function sexually in spite of their restrictive religious backgrounds. However, they add that many of these people never feel free to let themselves become involved sexually in an uninhibited way.

Homosexuality. Homosexual activity in the formative years is a major factor in the development of secondary impotence at a relatively youthful age. Of the 213 men referred for treatment of secondary impotence, twenty-one had homosexual experiences as teenagers,

---

[2] *HSI*, p. 179.

later married, and then rejected heterosexuality after marriage. Twelve of these men were in their twenties, seven were in their thirties, and only two were in their forties when they found themselves impotent with their wives.

None of these secondarily impotent men had ever participated in a heterosexual experience before his first homosexual one. The man whose first mature sexual experience is homosexual appears to be marked by it, even though he switches to heterosexual lovemaking. There may be some pattern imprinted on his behavior that cannot be erased. Both primarily and secondarily impotent men who had homosexual experiences as teenagers continued to think of themselves as homosexually oriented in their adult lives, even though many married.

Homosexual men sometimes marry for social or financial security and the ones who do this frequently have little genuine feeling for their wives. When they develop secondary impotence, one of two patterns becomes apparent. In the first, the male has fears of performance during courtship which eventually surface after marriage into a pattern of secondary impotence. The second type enters marriage with little difficulty in heterosexual functioning, only to find years later that men once again predominate in his sexual desires. Often he tries to lead both a heterosexual and a homosexual life only to find that the physical and emotional demands are overwhelming. At that point the man usually loses what little interest he has in his wife. As he withdraws from her, she usually follows the pattern of other wives whose husbands withdraw from them—they press for more sexual encounters. When this happens, the pressure on the man to perform may cause secondary impotence.

In therapy Masters and Johnson have found that wives of homosexual men tend to be very understanding. These men most often are good, kind, and considerate husbands, and most wives want to preserve their marriages even though their husbands have had homosexual relationships. The man often expresses in therapy a certain warmth for his wife and a feeling of wanting to maintain his marriage for reasons of family, business, and community image.

Physical Problems. Although the most frequent causes of secondary impotence are psychologic, Masters and Johnson point out that there are many possible physical causes as well. Their book lists the most important of these for physicians, but emphasizes that the various diseases, conditions, and drugs listed rarely cause impotence and are seldom related to impotence. Of the 213 secondarily impotent men seen, only seven had physical problems, three of which were successfully treated.

The complete physical and laboratory examinations for all patients showed that there might be a two- or threefold increase in the incidence of diabetes or a prediabetic condition among secondarily impotent patients than there is in the general male population. Fourteen such cases were diagnosed among impotent men referred for treatment. Another six were referred for treatment after the diagnosis of diabetes had been made. None of these men had the advanced diabetes that causes deterioration of the nervous system. Why they became impotent is not known.

Dr. Masters cautions that this does not necessarily mean that diabetic men are predisposed to impotence; there are just not enough data available to know. If a man is referred for secondary impotence, glucose tolerance tests for diabetes and preclinical diabetes are performed routinely. Careful control of clinical diabetes does not cure the secondary impotence. Once the pattern is established, the secondary impotence itself must be treated.

Other Causes. Foundation therapists treated six men whose secondary impotence was the direct result of inadequate counseling from various kinds of professional people. See Chapter 17, "Doctors and Other Therapists: Do They Always Help?" for a discussion of this problem.

There remain in the Masters and Johnson series twelve cases of secondary impotence for which there were no dominant causes. Likely, many factors, including the particular psychologic susceptibility of the individual, were involved.

Treatment of Impotence

Impotent men generally approach therapy believing that nothing can be done to help them; consequently, the Foundation therapists take special care to give them confidence in themselves and in the therapists as authorities who can help. Particular attention to the marriage relationship is necessary too, because often an impotent man views his wife as especially threatening to his self-confidence. She is the one person who knows the full extent of his failure; he may feel that he cannot be a man in her presence. A sexually frustrated woman will sometimes obtain revenge or justification of her shrewishness by spreading word of her husband's inadequacy to friends or belittling him in other ways. If this situation exists, the wife in treatment must be urged emphatically to cooperate.

Treatment of both primary and secondary impotence begins with the initial interview on the first day of the treatment program. It follows the same format whether the man is primarily or secondarily impotent. At the initial interview with the couple, the cotherapists direct them *not* to participate in any sexual activity without specific instructions. Immediately, treatment is underway because this directive serves to take the pressure to perform off the male partner. With performance fears somewhat abated, cotherapists and patients begin their joint exploration of the patients' marriage relationship during the roundtable discussion on Day Three. They also begin teaching the couple about natural sexual response and begin re-educating them about religious taboos, homosexuality, drinking, or whatever is relevant to the individuals in treatment.

The most important part of this educative process is to convince the male partner that he does not have to *do* anything to have an erection. Erection is a physiologic response that happens when effective sexual stimuli are present and when the man is psychologically prepared to respond to them. Masters and Johnson's approach is to convince the man that they can and will set conditions right so that he will feel sexual arousal and have erection.

During the roundtable discussion and on the day of the first sensate focus opportunities (see Chapter 8), the cotherapists explain to the couple why early sexual prohibitions and restrictions have such a strong influence on their sexual functioning now. Everyone mentally constructs for himself, from early childhood onward through adolescence and youth, a value system with regard to sexual activity. Sex can be thought of as beautiful or dirty, redeeming or sinful, pleasurable or painful, permissible in one situation but not in another. This value system affects, positively or negatively, an individual's natural physical capacity to function sexually. Sometimes the natural sexual drive is enough to overcome negative attitudes. In other instances it is not. Masters and Johnson feel it is especially important for the impotent man to understand the effect of his negative attitudes toward sex on his ability to function. Understanding these attitudes, they say, helps him to neutralize their harmful effects.[3]

Once a man is reassured about the total invalidity of religious prohibitions and is relieved of the burden of other myths and misconceptions, three basic problems must be overcome before he can function effectively: his performance fears must be removed; he must stop mentally watching himself during sexual activity, and his wife's fears for him must be relieved. How are these things to be accomplished? The sensate focus provides the way. It is usually begun after the roundtable discussions on the third or fourth day of therapy.

As the patients "pleasure" each other nonsexually in the first sensate focus period by caressing and stroking each other, the warmth and closeness created by this activity become the focus of their attention. There is no goal that a man must reach to be successful in this phase of treatment because the partners have been forbidden by the therapists to touch genital organs or to have intercourse. A man need not observe himself because there is nothing to watch for, and his wife has no fears for him because sexual performance is not expected. After a time or two at this kind of pleasuring, the man and woman can relax; they can give and take sensate pleasure, and they can begin to think and feel sexually.

---

[3] For a more complete discussion of sexual value systems, especially in relation to female sexual functioning, see Chapter 13.

On Day Four or Five the partners are asked again to pleasure each other, but this time, after caressing other parts of the body, they are specifically instructed to touch the genitals and the woman's breasts. Whatever either partner has learned from masturbating or other sexual experiences about his own sexual response is shared at this time with the other partner. If the husband does the pleasuring first, the wife guides him by placing her hand lightly over his as he fondles her. In that way she shows him, without the distraction of talking, what pleases her best. Then, the husband directs his wife, with his hand guiding hers to whatever genital stimulation is most exciting for him.

The couple should be positioned comfortably in bed, perhaps with the woman seated leaning against the headboard and the man lying on his back with his body between her legs and his legs spread apart over hers (Fig. 4). The man must tell his wife specifically how to stimulate his penis—how tightly to hold it, how quickly and how hard to rub it, and what areas are sensitive. For each partner to understand what pleases and what irritates the other is essential. Unfortunately, many people still consider this kind of communication undignified and shameful, but this attitude must be overcome.

During this stage of the therapy, the partners gradually give up their spectator roles and focus instead on giving pleasure to each other. This is especially important for the impotent man. When he forgets about watching for his own response and determines instead to give pleasure to his mate, he initiates what Masters and Johnson have called the "give to get" cycle. The impotent man must be taught to give of himself primarily for his wife's pleasure and then allow himself to be totally caught up in the warmth of her response. Through this process of giving and getting, sexual excitement builds in both partners.

In traditional therapy for impotence the time always arrives when the therapist suggests that the man should be ready to have intercourse. Even if the therapist tries not to put this in the form of a command, the patient almost invariably feels that he has to go all the way at once. All the old performance fears may come rushing back to inundate any natural response to sexual stimulation.

Therapy at the Foundation, however, is not pressured. If erection occurs, as it does usually during one of the pleasuring sessions, the couple *is not permitted* to rush to complete the performance. They are encouraged to use their times together to develop the ability to communicate with each other, continuing in the pleasuring session until erection occurs regularly, but not proceeding to complete intercourse. There is, of course, a tremendous accrual of sexual tensions built up this way which works to the therapists' advantage.

Once the man's erective pattern is established, he and his wife are directed to experiment with this response. Masters and Johnson emphasize this as the most effective step in the physical part of the program. The wife is instructed to "tease" the man's genitals in whatever ways she has learned are the most effective. When erection is firm, she stops playing, and they lie in each others arms until the erection goes away. She then repeats the process several times during at least a thirty-minute period. By use of the teasing technique, the man gradually overcomes the fear of losing his erection and not getting it back.

Whenever the cotherapists feel that the man is ready, usually within a week after the Day 3 roundtable, they give the couple instructions for the next step. During their next time together, after preliminary sex play, but before beginning manipulation of his penis, the wife is instructed to straddle her husband and seat herself on his thighs (Fig. 5). She begins by playing with the penis, finally stimulating it to full erection. Then, angling the penis toward herself, about forty-five degrees from the perpendicular, she directs entry. Masters and Johnson instruct the wife to insert the penis because she knows exactly where the entrance is; she can get over the possible awkward moment at which many erective failures occur. If she is poised above the man, stimulating the penis first, it is easy for her to insert it in a calm, unhurried way without the man's being distracted by having to move his body or find the entrance. During this learning period, the partners are encouraged to try entry several times in the female superior coital position until they can accomplish it with ease and confidence. The cotherapists assure the couple that if erection does not occur during one particular try, there is always another time.

Even though the partners are successful with erection and entry, a man may still fear that his erection will not stay hard enough to continue with intercourse. Especially if he senses any sexual demand from his partner, he may become fearful that the erection will not last long enough for her to have orgasm. If he notices a partial loss of erection caused by the distraction of fear, he panics, and complete loss of erection follows. To overcome this fear, the cotherapists explain to the wife that she must not at this stage move in a demanding way toward her climax.

Instead, after entry has been accomplished, the wife moves forward and backward slowly on the penis. She must not move demandingly, regardless of her own level of sexual tension. If the erection is lost, the wife merely needs to withdraw and manipulate the penis to erection again. After the wife has thrust slowly for a few minutes, she remains still and the man in turn tries thrusting gently so that he can experience the sensation of penile constriction and vaginal warmth. The husband should do this just as he would rub his wife's back or stroke her body during the sensate focus exercises. Because the partners have been told specifically not to move demandingly, there is no pressure to perform.

On the following days, the couple is again instructed to experience sensate and pelvic pleasuring of each other and then to go on to entry and slow pelvic thrusting using the female superior coital position. The husband's attention is turned to the warm, intimate, personally and sexually satisfying total situation. Foundation therapists *never* instruct a couple to proceed to climax. When orgasm does occur for either partner, it should not be by plan, but allowed to be a natural, involuntary happening.

Masters and Johnson are often asked whether most couples follow instructions willingly and correctly. They say that most patients are extremely attentive because the therapy program is set up so that they are rewarded as they progress. From the moment of their first physical improvement through communication during the sensate focus, the partners realize the importance of communication and the importance of following directions. While the patients' physical relationship is improving, the therapists are able to move in psychologically on the marital disharmony or whatever other negative attitudes are causing the sexual dysfunction. Masters declares, "This is action therapy. We use the physical changes just as you dangle candy before a youngster. While they're grabbing at the candy, we're treating the marital relationship."

The Foundation's approach to the impotent male, and in fact to all sexually dysfunctional people, is not oriented primarily to the physical instructions. These are the easiest part of the therapy to describe in a book, but really the basis of the Foundation program is building communication between the partners and re-educating them about sexual functioning. The positive personal interaction between the partners, with the cotherapists acting as a catalyst, makes the physical part of therapy succeed. This is why Masters and Johnson do not consider the program they have outlined as a set of "do-it-yourself" instructions that everyone can follow. Certainly some couples with sexual problems but with a good personal relationship may be able to help themselves after reading about the program, but for many others, treatment of their marriage relationship requires outside help.

Masters and Johnson have a special word of commendation for wives of impotent men. Usually they are extremely cooperative. Even if they arrive in St. Louis feeling hostile and revengeful, once they begin in therapy they give themselves fully and willingly to help their husbands.

Results of Treatment

More unmarried men were referred to the Foundation with the complaint of primary impotence than with any other sexual dysfunction. They were treated with either a replacement partner—that is, a woman of their choice who accompanied them to St. Louis for therapy, or a partner surrogate, a female partner whom the Foundation selected. (See Chapter 12, "Replacement Partners and Partner Surrogates.") Masters and Johnson called the primarily impotent male "the Foundation's clinical disaster area." Thirty-two men were treated. Of these, nineteen reversed their dysfunction, which means that 59.4 percent were successfully treated. Improvement in this success is likely, because nine treatment failures occurred in the first sixteen cases and only four in the last sixteen. The most difficult problems to treat were those of homosexuals and patients with fanatic religious backgrounds. Four of the six rigidly religious patients and two of the six homosexual patients who were primarily impotent could not be helped.

The secondarily impotent men responded better to treatment. Of 213 patients, 157 (73.8 percent) were treated successfully. Masters and Johnson's clinical techniques have been amazingly successful, especially considering the discouraging results of treatment from other forms of therapy.

CHAPTER 12

Replacement Partners and Partner Surrogates

A problem Masters and Johnson had to solve quickly when they began their therapy program in 1959 was what to do about the unmarried man or woman who wanted treatment. Since they felt that the best results could be achieved with a man and woman being treated together by a dual-sex team, would they have to accept marriage as a criterion for accepting or refusing patients who wanted help? The decided that they wanted to treat single people if single people could have just as much chance for successful therapy as a married couple. How could they arrange this? The solution to the problem, namely, allowing replacement partners and providing partner surrogates makes one of the most fascinating sections in *Human Sexual Inadequacy*.

A replacement partner is a person who is not married to the patient but with whom he or she has an ongoing sexual relationship. A partner surrogate is a third member of the therapy team, in addition to the two cotherapists, who acts as a sexual partner for the patient. Replacement partners are chosen by the man or woman who requests therapy. Thirteen men so far have brought women of their choice, and three women have gone through the two-week therapy program with men they had selected as sexual partners before treatment. These men and women had lived together as married couples and therefore were treated as a husband or a wife. Treatment of dysfunctional people with replacement partners was not a difficult problem. Because these people had lived together they came to St. Louis already attuned to the psychosexual side of their partners.

The real problems were to find partners for sexually inadequate people who had no spouse or replacement partner and to determine if such an arrangement would provide effective therapy. Here, Masters and Johnson made a distinction between male and female sexuality. They decided not to provide partner surrogates for women. When they set up their study criteria in 1958, they felt that a two-week treatment period would not be long enough to establish the personal relationship a sexually dysfunctional woman would need to be successful in therapy. As Mrs. Johnson says, "Women have been programmed for centuries to the concept of one man. If you look to fiction, poetry, the arts generally, you will find the picture of the woman pining in the tower for him."

Cultural attitudes toward female sexuality are slowly changing, however, and Mrs. Johnson has said recently that a woman who can accept her sexuality the way a man does, a woman who does not need the sanction of personal commitment to function sexually—that woman could be successful in therapy with a partner surrogate. The Foundation now in 1970 might accept such a patient provided an acceptable male surrogate could be found. Masters and Johnson do think that it will be more difficult to find acceptable men surrogates than women surrogates. They say men might want to be partner surrogates to "turn themselves on," and this would not be the right attitude for a therapeutic situation. "Women do not usually turn themselves on," Mrs. Johnson adds. "They may respond sexually, but they respond out of the emotional set of the surrogate situation more than out of the sexual act."

The Partner Surrogates

The role of the surrogates is to offer "someone to hold on to, talk to, work with, learn from, be a part of, and above all else, *give to* and *get from* during the sexually dysfunctional male's two weeks in the acute phase of therapy." [1] Masters and Johnson never considered hiring prostitutes for this role because, psychologically, it would have been destructive for the men. Thirteen women have served as surrogates over the past eleven years. Together with the cotherapists, they have treated forty-one men. The women range in age from twenty-four to forty-three years; three are over forty; all have at least a high-school education, and many have college and graduate degrees. All but two of the thirteen had been married in the past, and among the thirteen there are nine children. Ten are occupied full time in various careers, and some had been volunteers in the Foundation's physiologic studies. Surrogate partner volunteers were interviewed extensively by both a male and female Foundation therapist, singly and together. The realities of being a surrogate were honestly explored, and if there was any hesitancy on the part of an applicant, she was excluded immediately. Approximately sixty percent of

---
[1] *HSI*, p. 147.

of the women who applied as surrogate partners were rejected.

One might ask, why did these women volunteer? Many either had had sexual problems in their own marriages or were aware of some in their immediate families. These women were interested in offering their services because they had a strong personal interest in sexual dysfunctioning. Some women said they had no acceptable sexual opportunities and wanted the chance to relieve their own sexual tensions and the opportunity for a social relationship. Others volunteered because they wanted to help another person and felt themselves suited to the unusual challenge. One female physician volunteered, and she contributed enormously as a surrogate and as a professional who could offer constructive advice about therapeutic procedures.

All of the surrogates are well experienced sexually and are sexually well functioning. They are compassionate women interested in the welfare of their partners. Before participating in the program, they were thoroughly indoctrinated about male physiology and psychology, especially those aspects of the male's sexual performance that cause him anxiety. "These women know more about sexual function than most physicians," says Dr. Masters, adding, "It requires a woman who is unusually secure in her own female role to take on this task. We wouldn't dream of accepting anyone who wasn't perfectly comfortable and happy with her own sexuality. If she can't be at ease with herself, she can't be at ease with anyone else." However, no woman has been a surrogate more than once a year. Because the experience involves giving so much of one's self, it probably is not wise to subject a woman to it often.

The surrogate women are genuinely warm companionable individuals who perform an important part of their therapy even before becoming sexually involved with the male patients. At first the couple spends time relaxing together, going out to dinner or some other social activity. The surrogate puts the man at ease and lessens his anxiety about himself and the treatment program. Some partner surrogates spend evenings with male patients, but for others it is easier to see the patients during the day. The patients have considerable free time so schedules can be worked out individually.

The therapists try to match age, personality, and educational and social background in selecting a surrogate for a patient, but they are very careful not to let men "order up what they want." Offering a man exactly what he wanted in a partner surrogate would be doing him a disservice. If a patient were totally successful in therapy with "the ideal person," he would be at a disadvantage attempting a sexual liaison with someone else. Older men occasionally express a preference for a much younger surrogate, but the therapists feel that this too is a socially unrealistic situation, and they will not match people who differ widely in age. Care is also taken not to divulge personal details of the man's life to the surrogate, and the woman is advised not to discuss personal aspects of her own life with the patient. The aura of therapy is to be warm and responsive, but not romantic. Realistically, after therapy a man would expect to take up his own life pattern again without dependence on the surrogate.

Once the man feels secure with his partner, they move into the sexual phase of the therapy, which would be comparable to therapy for any husband and wife. Each woman is given detailed information about her prospective partner's case, and after therapy begins she is informed of progress daily.

Results of Treatment

A serious question was raised in the beginning of the program about whether or not the provision of sexual partners for patients would be good treatment. Now, twelve years later, the answer to this question is available —therapy results with replacement partners and partner surrogates were approximately those achieved with married couples. The men who brought to the Foundation women to whom they were not married had the usual inadequacies troubling married males. Four men with premature ejaculation were successfully treated; one primarily impotent man was relieved of his symptom and one was not; and five of the seven secondarily impotent males who brought replacement partners achieved symptom reversal. Of the three women treated with replacement partners, two had been married previously. None had ever had orgasm during intercourse, but with the cooperation of their male replacement partners two women of three achieved orgasm in therapy.

Many of the forty-one men who were treated with partner surrogates had been married at least once and divorced, because of sexual difficulties. It is worth noting the specifics of these men's inadequacies and what happened after rapid therapy. Twelve had premature ejaculation; one could not ejaculate; nineteen were primarily impotent; and nine were secondarily impotent. All the men with ejaculation problems had their symptoms reversed by therapy with surrogates. Twelve of the primarily impotent males and seven of the secondarily impotent men were also treated successfully, for a total of thirty-two treatment successes.

What happens to these men when they return home and their surrogate partner is no longer available? Each patient is told ahead of time that it would help him if he had someone with whom he could make a sexual liaison. The potential to function effectively is there if a man can place his new knowledge and awareness into the context of his own life pattern, but he must use this potential or risk becoming inadequate again. Of the thirty-two men who were treated successfully with partner surrogates, twenty-four are now married, and only one, a man with secondary impotence, has reverted to the dysfunctional state.

CHAPTER 13

Orgasmic Dysfunction in Women

Understanding Sexual Function

What makes people sexually capable, sexually incapable, or varying degrees in between? Masters and Johnson have worked out a conceptual way of understanding sexual functioning as an interaction between two sexual systems—the biophysical and the psychosocial. Strong negative signals from either system result in dysfunction for an individual of either sex. Because of the double standard, however, women receive a disproportionate number of negative signals about sex, and that is why it is especially important to understand the two systems in relation to female sexuality.

Obviously, the biophysical system—a reasonably healthy body and anatomically functional sex organs—must be present. But what of the other, the psychologic and social components of sexual function? There is, for every individual, a psychosocial system—a set of values and attitudes relating to sex—which interacts with the biophysical system.

These systems are capable of reinforcing each other; the naturally occurring biophysical sex urge is enhanced if the person regards sexual feelings as valuable, acceptable and worthy of expression. Likewise, positive attitudes toward sex can go a long way toward overcoming deficiencies in the biophysical system. The sexual behavior of many women after the birth of a baby is an example of the psychosocial system's positive influence on the biophysical. Even though women are not physically normal until several weeks after delivery, many want sexual activity and say that they enjoy it as much as before. Their positive attitudes win the day, even though their hormones aren't working right and the baby has kept them up all night.

But what if a person has not had the opportunity or the information with which to construct a positive value system about sex? Worse yet, what if everything a child or young person growing up has heard or been taught about sex is negative? Of course, in these instances, the signals from the psychosocial system will exert a negative influence on sexual functioning. Both sexes need positive signals from both systems to be sexually capable. To this extent, the sexual problems of men and women have similar sources.

However, what if society in general accepts sexual functioning in one sex as natural and places a high value on it, while rejecting the idea of naturally occurring sexuality in the other? Individuals of both sexes have been victims of isolation, ignorance, and repression, but in our culture only the female has been forbidden to accept herself honorably as a sexual being. Many girls as they grow up, even now, deny their sexual feelings in order to conform to society's image of "proper" behavior for girls.

> During her formative years the female dissembles much of her developing functional sexu-

ality in response to societal requirements for a "good girl" façade. Instead of being taught or allowed to value her sexual feelings in anticipation of appropriate and meaningful opportunity for expression, thereby developing a realistic sexual value system, she must attempt to repress or remove them from their natural context of environmental stimulation under the implication that they are bad, dirty, etc. She is allowed to retain the symbolic romanticism which usually accompanies these sexual feelings, but the concomitant sensory development with the symbolism that endows the sexual value system with meaning is arrested or labeled—for the wrong reasons—objectionable.[1]

Boys, on the other hand, even if their individual families are restrictive, are allowed by the culture to accept their sexuality. Emotionally, if not intellectually, they learn to recognize and to value the factors which enhance it.

Masters and Johnson have observed that both men and women, perhaps surprisingly, place a high value in their psychosocial systems on personal identification, affection, and respect as factors which are necessary for enjoyable sexual performance. Only men, however, have societal permission to function sexually which they can take for granted. Thus, the components of their value systems remain obscure unless sexual dysfunction makes it necessary to discover what is missing. In other words, men may never consciously realize that they need warmth, tenderness, and identification with their partners to function effectively. Women, on the other hand, do not have society's permission to be sexual beings. They feel that they need special permission for sexuality,

---
[1] *HSI*, pp. 215-216.

so they spell out more specifically the conditions under which they are allowed, or will allow themselves, to have sexual experience. Society's denial of female sexuality, "the double standard," forces many women into highly restrictive and unrealistic value systems, systems which can be so confining that they do not allow the woman to function at all. An extreme example is, "Sex is dirty but must be tolerated once in a while in order to have children."

Another effective barrier to female responsiveness, also related to the double standard, is the idea that it is a woman's duty to satisfy her husband. If the woman herself accepts this idea and tries only to accommodate the man, she inhibits her own response. This also tends to deprive him of a meaningful stimulus which her response could provide. A man who thinks it is his wife's duty to satisfy him, and who proceeds in the sex act as if she were physically but not psychically present, is inhibiting also. He denies the woman's sexuality and refuses to recognize that she has the same needs for physical satisfaction that he does. He may think that his excitement should be enough to carry her along. However, Masters and Johnson's earlier studies of the human sexual response make it obvious that this is not true. Women (and men too) need to be sexually stimulated in ways which are personally exciting and acceptable. A highly excited man is certainly capable of bringing a highly excited woman to orgasm without thinking about how he is doing it, but if the woman feels no sexual tension, his excitement alone will not be enough.

Until *Human Sexual Response* was published in 1966, there were no large-scale observations of the female's physiologic response to sexual stimulation and her capability of having orgasm. These studies, which demonstrated the sexual capacity of women, added to Masters and Johnson's contact with women in treatment of sexual problems, have shown them clearly the role of our culture in inhibiting female sexuality. Their comment on the situation is too startling to repeat in any but their own words.

> Yet, woman's conscious denial of biophysical capacity rarely is a completely successful venture, for her physiological capacity for sexual response infinitely surpasses that of man. Indeed, her significantly greater susceptibility to negatively based psychosocial influences may imply the existence of a natural state of psychosexual-social balance between the sexes that has been *culturally established* [italics added] to neutralize woman's biophysical superiority.[2]

Masters and Johnson readily admit the speculative nature of their statement, adding that if it is true, then it is obvious that women have been a party to the establishment and maintenance of this balance in the interest of sustaining men's confidence in their ability to be sexually effective.

Women Who Have Never Had Orgasm

"Primary orgasmic dysfunction" is not a term analogous to primary impotence. "Primarily impotent" describes a man who has never had a hard enough erection to have intercourse when the opportunity is available. Most of these men masturbate or are manipulated to ejaculation regularly—they have experienced orgasm,

---
[2] *HSI*, pp. 219-220.

but not during coitus. A woman with primary orgasmic dysfunction has never had orgasm by any method. Masters and Johnson do not use the word "frigidity." Dr. Masters explains, "We don't know what it means. It doesn't mean anything. It means a woman who doesn't have orgasm, and it means a woman who has orgasm once a week and her husband thinks she ought to have it twice. So we never use it." Mrs. Johnson adds, "As far as I am concerned it's slang, and poor slang. Some male who thinks of women only as sex objects must have affixed it because it is not a term that a woman would apply to a variation of her own response."

There are so many possible causes for orgasmic dysfunction, so many possible influences on a woman's biological capacity and psychosocial values, that it is impossible to list them. In *Human Sexual Inadequacy* cases which typify the most frequent circumstances associated with orgasmic dysfunction in women are reported. In summary, some of these follow.

Religious Prohibitions. Of the 193 women treated at the Foundation for primary orgasmic dysfunction, forty-one were from rigidly religious families. People from all the major religious groups in the nation participated in this disaster—eighteen patients were from Catholic homes, sixteen from Jewish, and seven from fundamentalist Protestant families. The destructiveness of denial and repression backed by religious sanctions is decisively evident.

Sex equaled sin in the family of one young woman who was referred to the Foundation with her husband because they had not been able to consummate their marriage in nine years.

"Cold, formal, and controlled" were the words Masters and Johnson used to describe this woman's childhood. Every day prolonged family prayers were punctuated with the father's edicts which covered all aspects of life. Sex was absolutely never mentioned, and the father censored and selected all books, newspapers, and radio programs. The patient recalled her mother as a seemingly emotionally devoid person whose reasons for living were centered around household tasks and serving her husband.

After graduation from a denominational college, the patient worked as a secretary for a publisher of religious books. There she met a young man whose religious upbringing was almost the same as hers. The whole of their physical courtship consisted of three kisses. On the wedding day, her mother instructed her that it was now her duty to serve her husband and to allow him "privileges" (unspecified). She was also told unequivocally that her husband would hurt her, although "it" would stop hurting after a while. The most significant point in the instructions, however, was that "good women" do not show any "interest in the thing."

The wedding night was an extended nightmare, with the inexperienced husband trying to locate the vagina, while the bride struggled to keep as covered up as possible. Of course, the husband's panicky efforts hurt, just as her mother had said they would. In all the nine years of their marriage, as the husband's approaches dwindled from once nightly to once every three or four months, she never got the idea that she should cooperate with his efforts. Her feeling was that since this experience was for his enjoyment only, her husband would have to manage it on his own. His attempts to consummate the marriage evoked from her only pain, which never somehow went away and finally a complete rejection of sex in general and her husband in particular.

Both husband and wife needed extensive education and reorientation of their psychosocial values. Incredible as it may appear, this woman was able to have orgasm during the two-week treatment period.

"The thing that's fascinating us now," comments Mrs. Johnson about the case just related, "is that we've had a fairly even thread of the kind of people who reflect major social and emotional deprivation. They recall no one who has held, loved, touched or rewarded them in an emotional sense. And they find one another." Dr. Masters adds, "Two emotional negatives don't make a positive. It takes someone like Gini to help develop something positive out of a relationship like that."

A Protective Vacuum. Occasionally, say Masters and Johnson, a women arrives at physical maturity without developing enough emotional maturity for female identification and development of a sexual value system. They relate the story of an only child, born relatively late to rather emotionally restrained parents, who "became the doll they dressed exquisitely, handled little, and disregarded emotionally." She could not recall having decided anything for herself until her second year of college, when she became engaged to a man seven years older than she. He had been brought up by an older aunt and uncle, and had had little opportunity to learn about personal relationships. Although he was very restrained in his life style, he had no negative attitudes toward sex. The couple had two children during the eleven years of their marriage before referral to the Foundation, but the wife had never had orgasm. She had, however, made many active attempts, including finally treatment at the Foundation, to improve the quality of the couple's sexual relations.

Once under treatment the husband responded

remarkably, his restraint giving way to a warmly demonstrative and communicative role. The wife, unfortunately, in spite of her enthusiasm for the treatment program and her good relationship with her husband, remained nonorgasmic. No specific events in her history except lack of opportunity for development can be cited as the cause of this woman's strong block against sexual expression.

The "Second-Best" Mate. Probably the most frequent cause of orgasmic dysfunction is inability of the woman to identify with her partner. If in her eyes he is a social bore, a financial failure, a slob, a perfectionist, or "the second-best man," enough negative signals from the psychosocial system may be generated to make trouble.

A wife with three teenage children who could not identify with her mate was referred to the Foundation for treatment because she had never had orgasm. When she was twenty-two and working as a secretary, she became engaged to a young salesman. She had an excellent relationship with him; from the history it appeared that they not only were "in love" in the romantic sense but that they also shared goals and interests. She was highly aroused by petting with him but never had orgasm although he ejaculated regularly in response to her manipulation.

Plans had been made for the wedding, but three weeks before, while the intended groom was on a business trip, he met a divorcée with two children and married her one week later. The young girl was stricken. She had made a total commitment to her fiancé and he had been the only man to whom she had ever formed an intense attachment.

In six months she married another man whom she

described as "kind and considerate," but who had very little sexual experience and no idea of how to be effective with his wife. From her viewpoint their sex life was adequate but not nearly as exciting as her experiences with her former fiancé. She could not help having fantasies of her first love during sexual relations with her husband, and these were enough to prevent her from having orgasm.

Her husband, as the years went by, was forced to bear the blame for her problem. In time she became dissatisfied with his income and his position in the community. As it happened, her former fiancé's achievements in business and other areas brought him local prominence, and her husband came off badly by comparison. Psychiatric treatment did not help this woman, and eventually the couple came to the Foundation for treatment.

Therapy centered around helping her to identify with her husband and helping her to recognize the immaturity of idolizing the man who had jilted her years ago. Having the female cotherapist to present the husband's good character traits as she saw them was extremely important in treating this woman and is an effective technique generally in helping women who are having trouble identifying with their husbands. Treatment also provided education in the techniques of effective sexual stimulation for the husband. Masters and Johnson say that chances for success are very good in such cases.

Marriage to a Sexually Inadequate Man. The idea that in any sexual interaction pressure is on the man to perform, while the woman needs only to make herself physically available, was discussed in the chapter on impotence. That is true—for physical connection to be made, the man has to have an erection. However, when one considers the requirements for female *response* (not just submission), a woman's situation can be extremely difficult if her partner has any kind of sexual problem. She loses the opportunity to be involved sexually in a free and uninhibited way when she also must be concerned with her partner's adequacy in his role. Performance fears for her partner can stop her from responding. Furthermore, the male partner must have and maintain a reasonably adequate erection for the female to reach a climax during intercourse. In contrast, a man can experience arousal and have orgasm during coitus without any sexual response from his partner. Masters and Johnson stress this point because many of the women they treated who had never had orgasm were married to men with sexual problems.

This was the situation of a women in her twenties married to a man who was sixteen years older than she. She was the eldest of three children whose father had died when they were young. After high-school graduation, the girl had gone to work to help support the family. During high school and afterward she dated and had many petting experiences but never tried to have intercourse. She also experimented with masturbation a few times but never had orgasm.

She married her husband because he was well off financially, and she saw marriage as a chance to escape from poverty and to help the two younger children. Actually, she was rather surprised at her fiancé's lack of sexual interest during their engagement, but she did not know that he had serious sexual problems.

During the honeymoon she found he was impotent. She tried to help him by stimulating him in many ways, following his directions, but did not succeed. About six months after the wedding the husband woke up with an erection. Without any preliminaries he moved over, put his penis into his wife's vagina and ejaculated quickly. It hurt a little but she responded positively, feeling that this at least was progress. Unfortunately, in the four years of their marriage before their referral for treatment there was no more progress. Episodes like the one just described occurred a few times a year, but the husband never had an erection unless he awoke with one. She never experienced orgasm even though her husband tried oral-genital and manual stimulation.

A woman married to a man who ejaculates prematurely is also at an extreme disadvantage vis-à-vis her own sexual satisfaction. Every coital experience is over before she has a chance to respond. After the first few episodes of being left with her physical needs unsatisfied, she begins to fear the too-quick conclusion of any sexual encounter. She may be completely capable of responding fully and having orgasm a short time after the penis is in her vagina. Instead, as soon as thrusting begins, she tries to hurry her own response; she fears that she won't succeed and is so distracted by fear that her sexual tension dissipates altogether. Eventually she begins to feel that her husband is using her without really caring for her as a person. The negative feelings created by this situation are strong enough to dispel her naturally occurring sexual tension. Masters and Johnson treated 223 couples in which both partners complained of sexual problems. The most frequent combined problems were premature ejaculation and orgasmic dysfunction—107 marriages.

Situational Orgasmic Dysfunction

Some women can have orgasm with masturbation, with partner manipulation or with oral-genital stimulation, but not during intercourse. Masters and Johnson call this "coital orgasmic inadequacy." The reverse situation also happens. A woman may be orgasmic during intercourse but not with other kinds of stimulation. This is called "masturbatory orgasmic dysfunction." There are also women who had had orgasm at least once during both manipulative and coital episodes but are dysfunctional when referred for treatment because their attitudes toward their partners have changed or because they are homosexually oriented. Some of these women actually have little interest in sex altogether and rarely have orgasm; they may be able to reach climax while on a vacation or in some other special situation. This is called "random orgasmic inadequacy." The entire group of problems—coital, masturbatory, and random orgasmic inadequacy—is referred to as "situational orgasmic dysfunction."

Does She Like Him? A woman's attitudes toward her partner exert an important influence on her sexual response to him. His masculinity, his intelligence, his character traits, his appearance, his drive, any number of variables, have to fit with the requirements of the woman's psychosocial value system for her to respond sexually. Furthermore, a woman's attitudes toward a man may change during the course of the relationship, as the following case history of a woman with situational orgasmic dysfunction shows.

The couple had been married twenty-three years

when they were referred for treatment. The wife had been orgasmic and sometimes multiorgasmic during the first twelve years of the marriage. But in the twelfth year, the husband was fired from the company for which he had worked successfully since the wedding. For eighteen months he was unable to find a permanent position; he became depressed and began to drink excessively, and the frequency of their sexual activity decreased. Vituperative arguments followed the wife's discovery that her husband was having an affair. She insisted on separate bedrooms.

For about six months the couple had no sexual contact, but during that time the husband found himself a permanent job, quit drinking, and stopped seeing the other woman. However, after the six-month separation, the wife discovered that she was no longer sexually responsive to her husband and that she could not have orgasm. She had stopped seeing him as a man, had lost confidence in him and respect for him. His drinking, his affair, his inability to get a decent job had changed her feelings about him as a person. Her psychosocial value system sent enough negative signals to stop her from responding to him sexually.

Homophile Orientation. Many women have had relatively long-lasting and significant homosexual relationships while they were teenagers. Having first reached orgasm in their sexual relations with other women, they find themselves dysfunctional in heterosexual relationships. In their psychosocial value system a male is basically an unacceptable partner.

This was the problem of a rather introverted young girl who had been seduced at fifteen years of age by a female teacher. During an increasingly intimate relationship, she gradually responded sexually with the teacher and eventually became multiorgasmic with mutual manipulation and oral-genital contact.

The relationship ended traumatically several years later when the teacher was caught making advances to other girls. She was fired and moved to a distant city. Physical separation and, above all, knowledge of the other's infidelity were too much for the girl to cope with. She became depressed and completely antisocial. Because of frequent episodes of depression, she saw a psychiatrist who was very helpful in encouraging her to find friends and to date. She had never dated heterosexually in high school or college, but curiosity led her to try heterosexual intercourse when she was twenty-five. The young man's far from subtle approach repelled her and she found herself comparing him unfavorably to her female lover.

The next year she met a man who had been divorced for several months. They were both lonely, and they shared several interests. An affectionate and warm relationship developed between them, and eventually they married. The husband was sexually knowledgeable besides being kind, considerate, and gentle, and she genuinely enjoyed giving him pleasure, but she never had orgasm. Her guilt about her homosexual relationship and her fear that she could never be heterosexually effective led her to insist on treatment after seven years of marriage.

"Just Not Interested in Sex." Masters and Johnson feel that it is possible for a person to have naturally occurring low sexual tension without a negative sexual value system, as reflected in the following case report of a husband who insisted that he and his wife be referred for treatment after eleven years of marriage. The wife had only two orgasms in her life, once with intercourse and once during manipulation. The husband was extremely frustrated by his wife's lack of responsiveness. Her rejoinder was that she was "just not interested in sex."

Virtually nothing about her background was remarkable. During her young adulthood, plenty of sexual opportunities were present that another woman would have found socially acceptable, but she was uninterested. She had no feelings about sex being shameful or dirty, but she felt that getting involved would be pointless.

More than a dozen years after college graduation, at age thirty-six, she married a man of thirty-three who worked in the same field. They started a business of their own. As Masters and Johnson put it, "From Mrs. H.'s point of view the marriage was simply another form of the business merger." Although his wife liked him as a person, the husband could never arouse her sexually, and she was sometimes even amused at his efforts to do so. To him this situation was completely frustrating and depressing.

One evening, about eighteen months before they came to the Foundation, the wife became very excited during intercourse and had orgasm. Both partners were surprised and elated. Unfortunately, this success was repeated only once more, this time during manipulation —and interestingly, on the night after a successful business deal had been concluded.

Masturbatory Orgasmic Inadequacy. Of the 149 women Masters and Johnson treated for situational orgasmic dysfunction only eleven could not masturbate or be manipulated to orgasm. The histories of these women follow either of two patterns. A young girl may try masturbation even though she feels guilty about it, then stop trying after a few failures. Later her guilt feelings prevent her from being responsive to this kind of stimulation, but she responds normally during intercourse.

The other situation is that of a little girl taught not to touch herself because it is sinful. She will avoid masturbation entirely throughout childhood and adolescence, and although she may reach orgasm during intercourse, she cannot have orgasm with manipulation or oral-genital contact.

Treatment of Orgasmic Dysfunction

Masters and Johnson say the circumstances associated with orgasmic dysfunction are extremely variable, and they must structure the therapy to meet each couple's needs. The psychotherapeutic component of treatment for the dysfunctional female is based upon two sources of information which indicate the woman's attitudes toward sex, the degree of her open-mindedness, and her physical responsiveness.

The first source of information is the history taken during the first few days of the program. The therapists must identify those things about the husband that do not match the requirements of his wife's existing sexual value system. These may be relatively trivial and easily correctable, such as, "He doesn't take a bath often enough, but I can't tell him." Or they may involve more basic issues. For example, the woman may have had better sex with other partners; she may have idyllic notions about sex which are unattainable in reality; she may have had traumatic sexual experiences; she may expect sex to be unpleasant; or she may think of it as dirty—all these stack the cards against her being receptive to her partner. Some of these attitudes may have to be reversed or at least neutralized.

The other source of information is what the patients report to the cotherapists each day after the sex homework sessions. As explained in Chapter 8, these discussions show whether or not the husband's physical approach is pleasing to the woman, or to put it in another way, the discussions show how well or how poorly the requirements of the woman's sexual value system are being met. The past history is tremendously important, but it does not provide a basis for treatment; it helps the therapists interpret what is happening in therapy from day to day. The daily interactions of the patients, and the mirror images of themselves presented by the therapists, comprise the material which is used directly in therapy.

The first goal of the therapists for a couple who have come for treatment of orgasmic dysfunction is to help them to stop behaving toward each other in hostile or otherwise negative ways, so that they can create an aura in their relationship that will be erotic. At the roundtable on Day Three the therapists reflect to the patients information from their histories which shows the couple which of their behaviors are destructive. When the husband and wife see themselves through the eyes of two objective but sympathetic outsiders they begin to realize the futility of antagonistic behaviors and to set them aside. During the discussion, the therapists also provide information about sex to counter myths and misunderstandings that stand in the way of the woman's response to sexual stimuli.

If the roundtable discussion goes well, the couple is given instructions in the sensate focus. (See Chapter 8.) With hostile, inhibiting, tension-provoking actions eliminated and superstitions about sex replaced with facts, the partners proceed in the first sensate opportunities, to learn about each other's responses to touching and caressing. The woman has an opportunity to discover, perhaps for the first time in her life, what is sexually arousing for her. Her sexuality, because it is accepted by the therapists who are authority figures, can now be accepted by the woman herself. She need no longer conform to the image of woman as a nonsexual creature. Masters and Johnson put it nicely:

> . . . the crucial factors most often missing in the sexual value system of the nonorgasmic woman are the pleasure in, the honoring of, and the privilege to express need for sexual experience. In essence, the restoration of sexual feeling to its appropriate psychosocial context (the primary focus of therapy for the nonorgasmic woman) is the reversal of sexual dissembling.[8]

After their first sensate focus sessions the couple's reactions to them are explored in the therapy session the next day. Discussing the behavior of the husband is especially important to find out if anything in his manner is inhibiting or destructive to the relationship. The woman must have a chance to communicate what she likes and what she dislikes without "anger, fear or frustration," say Masters and Johnson. The idea is to provide a warm, nondemanding, companionable atmosphere, an atmosphere in which the woman has the opportunity to think and feel sexually.

On Days Four and Five, after the partners have experienced feelings of closeness and intimacy in pleas-

---

[8] *HSI*, p. 298.

uring each other, they proceed to genital play. Here again the therapists provide not only details of positioning, approach, and timing but they also give psychologic permission for the woman to enjoy the fondling and manipulation of genital organs and to lose herself in this pleasure. Most important, they teach the man how to encourage the woman to show him what she wants rather than just let him do what he thinks she wants.

The most effective position for teaching genital play that stimulates the woman is for the man to sit, leaning against pillows at the head of the bed with the woman seated between his legs leaning with her back against his chest, and resting her head on one of his shoulders. She separates her legs and extends them across her husband's legs (Fig. 7). This position provides a warm and secure feeling for her. It gives the husband access to any part of her body to be explored using the principles of sensate focus. The wife is instructed to place her hand lightly over her husband's so that she can signal him to touch more lightly, more heavily, or in a different place. The wife can communicate her wishes directly in a physical way without having to talk.

An erection or any naturally occurring expression of male excitement is therapeutic for the wife. However, the husband must not, at this point, lose sight of the goal of the exercise and begin to second-guess his wife's desires or begin to stimulate her by using his choice of approach. The husband must not assume the role of the expert, because if he does there will be no opportunity for both husband and wife to discover what the *woman's* actual preferences are. When the husband and wife have learned from "controlled genital play" what techniques are effective, they can proceed to try out stimulative techniques of the man's choosing.

Figure 7. Comfortable position for female stimulation.

The cotherapists also instruct the husband specifically how to stimulate his wife during genital play episodes. Masters and Johnson say the biggest mistake most men make is to manipulate the clitoral glans (head of the clitoris) as soon as sex play is begun. The clitoris both receives stimuli and transmits them. Touching it produces a high level of excitement quickly. If this happens before the woman is psychologically ready, the cycle of effective stimulation is broken. In addition, the clitoral glans is sensitive to touch, and direct manipulation of it may be irritating or painful. When women masturbate they usually stroke the clitoral shaft rather than the glans.

Masters and Johnson say that probably the most effective approach is for the man to begin with gentle stroking and pleasuring of his partner. He continues with a light, teasing touch, feeling the woman's breasts and belly, moving to her thighs, then teasing at the vaginal outlet and moving back to the thighs, belly and breasts. It is best to avoid the clitoral area at first.

Then, to develop a pleasurable pelvic feeling for the woman, the man should manipulate the general area of the clitoris, especially the sides of the clitoral shaft. Stroking the insides of the thighs and the lips of the vagina is also erotic for most women. The pressure, the direction, and the rapidity of this stimulation is controlled by the woman with her hand overriding the man's. This frees her from having to adjust to stimulation which may not be exciting to her and also teaches her husband what her preferences are.

The man must remember that no lubrication is secreted by the clitoris. As the woman becomes sexually aroused, however, there will be lubricating material at the vaginal outlet. The man should insert a finger a little way into the vagina and then spread the vaginal lubrication in the clitoral area. This will prevent irritation from manipulation of a dry surface. In addition, the maneuver itself is stimulating. Most women, however, do not find deep penetration of the vagina with the fingers to be erotic.

There must be no demand on the man's part for the woman to reach orgasm. The purpose of this exercise is to give the woman a chance to focus on her own sexual feelings, to discover what her preferences are, and to communicate this information to her husband. The effectiveness of any one session is by no means lost if the woman does not reach a climax. In fact, the opposite is true. When the woman knows that nothing is demanded of her, that she has complete freedom to express herself, and that she will soon have another chance for sexual activity, there is a buildup of sexual feeling that eventually will result in climax. The mechanism that sets off the orgasmic response is unknown, but Masters and Johnson emphasize that it is a response which is impossible to will or to force. Orgasm just happens when the maximum amount of erotic stimuli for that particular woman is accumulated.

From the beginning of the sensate focus to the end of the treatment period, all directions to the couple to progress from one phase to the next are based on results reported by the couple in the daily sessions with the therapists. This means that there is no "schedule" for the introduction of new material. Husbands and wives who have never communicated with each other and couples who have long-standing problems will take longer to react positively to therapy than couples who do communicate and whose dysfunction has been brief. Masters and Johnson point out that partners who have adjusted to their dysfunction may resist reversal and need more time to develop sensate focus and become responsive during genital play. The point is that each "exercise" or phase in the treatment program is practiced until the goal of that particular exercise is reached. Each time a new exercise or technique is taught, the cotherapists urge the patients not to forget about the earlier ones. Each technique taught to the couple is employed in every sexual encounter so that a sexual response pattern is gradually built up and put together.

Usually a few days after the roundtable, the partners report that the woman has been aroused by the genital play episodes. The therapists then direct the couple to try insertion of the penis with the woman in the superior position (Fig. 5). The object is to get the woman to carry over the excitement accrued from genital play to an experience which includes feeling the penis in her vagina. In their next practice session, when the man has a full erection and the woman is well lubricated, if they feel a strong desire to continue, the man lies on his back, and the women kneels over him and inserts his penis. She is instructed to hold herself still so that she can appreciate the pleasurable feeling of vaginal dilation without any demand to reach a climax. As her sexual tension elevates and she finds that she wants more stimulation, she can move slowly back and forth on the penis for a brief time. The cotherapists tell the woman to think of the penis as hers to play with, to feel and to enjoy. A few trials of this exercise may be necessary before the woman develops vaginal feeling. The husband's role at this time is to provide an erect organ for his wife to play with.

Only after pleasurable or sexually demanding feeling

develops vaginally for the woman, perhaps a few days later in the treatment program, is the man instructed to try pelvic thrusting slowly and in a nondemanding manner. The wife is instructed to communicate to her partner the pace she prefers. Keeping the man from thrusting as quickly as he might otherwise provides the woman with a chance to feel what is happening rather than just trying to accommodate to her husband's pattern.

At this stage in the treatment program many men ask, "What if I feel like ejaculating?" The cotherapists emphasize constantly that learning ejaculatory control is both possible and desirable, and that it increases sexual pleasure for both partners. The spontaneous occurrence of a climax for either partner is not a problem. The cotherapists assure the couple ahead of time that it may happen and that they should just enjoy it. If it does happen, they are asked to follow the original instructions at their next opportunity. Actually, the therapists instruct the woman to manipulate her husband to ejaculation during the treatment period when he needs it. Otherwise, he probably could not cooperate in the deliberately tension-producing situations set up by the therapists.

In subsequent sessions, as the husband develops ejaculatory control and the wife develops vaginal feeling, the couple is instructed to try insertion of the penis with slow thrusting for as long as it is pleasurable. They then separate and lie in each other's arms, returning to the kinds of pleasuring they learned previously. When they feel aroused again, they reinsert the penis and repeat the episode. The timing of this generally is whatever is acceptable to both partners. The usual pattern of demanding pelvic thrusting initiated by either partner must be broken. If the husband initiates it, the wife must accommodate and thus lose her chance to respond; if the wife initiates it, she is usually trying to force her response. If the wife is convinced that the penis is hers just as the vagina is her husband's, she will play with it and enjoy it, allowing it to stimulate her just as she enjoyed the earlier pleasuring techniques.

Once the woman can enjoy having the penis inserted when she is in the female superior position, the couple is taught to convert this position to a lateral coital position. For an illustration of this position and an explanation of how to convert to it from the female superior position, see Figure 5 and p. 120.

Although every fourth day in the two-week treatment period is a "holiday" from sex, the conferences between the cotherapists and the patients continue in an effort to explore the marriage relationship in depth. With improvement of the physical problem, the couple is usually amenable and vulnerable to treatment of the marriage relationship itself. Sources of disaffection, disharmony, and dislike are explored. This is a tremendous help to the wife because communicating with her husband and getting along better with him make it much more likely that she will respond to him sexually.

Masters and Johnson emphasize the importance of the husband's attitude in the therapy of the nonorgasmic woman. There is no place for impatience, hostility or even indifference. As they put it:

> If he is totally cooperative, interested, supportive, and identifies quietly and warmly with his wife as she lives through the strain of the interpretive look in the mirror provided by the cotherapists,

her chances of orgasmic attainment are significantly increased.[4]

The wife can be assisted by the therapists to understand her own attitudes and to recognize her own desires. If she feels her husband's interest in her and his concern for her as a person, success is likely.

Always cautious in reporting their success, Masters and Johnson said that they were unable to help sixty-six (19.3 percent) of the 342 women treated during the two-week program. In some of these cases a destructive marital relationship could not be healed. When one considers, however, that orgasmic dysfunction is still thought to be untreatable by many physicians, their successes with four of every five women is truly astonishing. Only five reversals to a dysfunctional state took place among the 137 women who were treated five years ago or more, proving beyond doubt the efficacy and value of the method.

---

[4] *HSI*, p. 313.

CHAPTER 14

Vaginismus

Masters and Johnson have treated twenty-nine women who had an unusual psychosomatic illness called "vaginismus." Any sexual approach to a woman with vaginismus causes an involuntary tightening or spasm (*ismus*, spasm) in the outer third of the vagina (Fig. 8). The spastic contraction can be so severe that it is impossible for the woman to have intercourse. Foundation therapists have treated one couple who did not have intercourse for the first fourteen years of their marriage because of this disorder.

Diagnosis of Vaginismus

Psychotherapists cannot be sure from an interview whether vaginismus is present or not. A definite diagnosis can be made only by examination; in fact, these women have a characteristic reaction to the examination or even to the examiner's approach. Usually they will attempt to slide up to the head of the examining table away from the doctor, even taking their feet out of the stirrups and holding their legs together. While

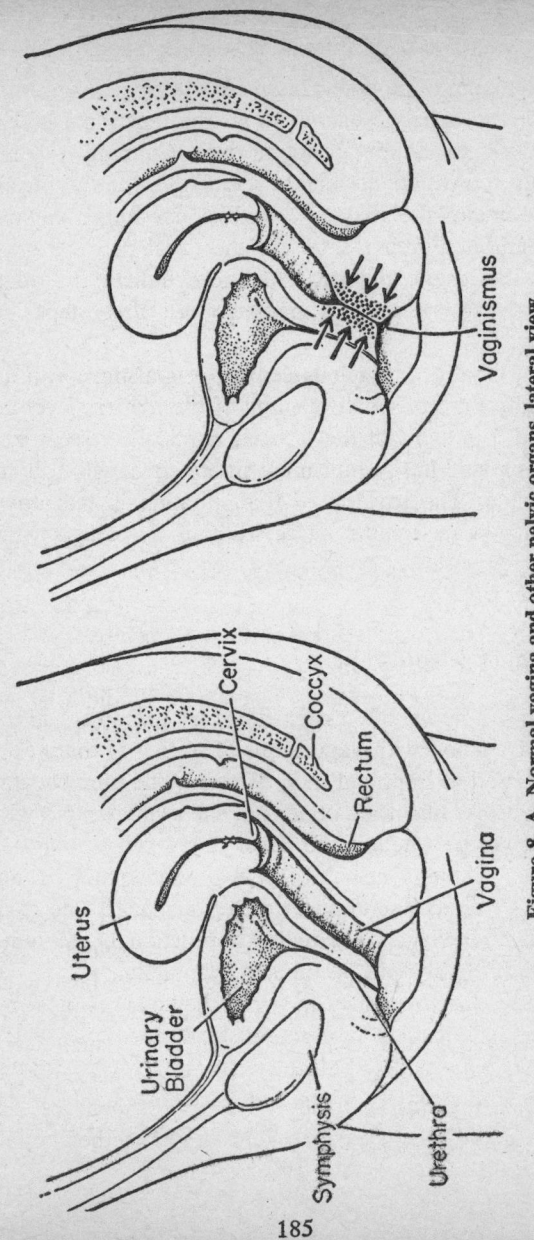

Figure 8. A, Normal vagina and other pelvic organs, lateral view. B, Vaginismus (involuntary constriction of outer third of vagina).

some tenseness and embarrassment are frequent normal reactions to a pelvic examination, the reaction of literally trying to escape is not normal. Calming and reassuring these patients makes it possible for the physician to make the diagnosis with a one-finger vaginal examination. Forcing entry for the usual pelvic examination can make the problem more difficult to treat, wheras reassurance and patience are first steps in therapy.

Occasionally, physicians confuse vaginismus with an unusually tight or small opening of the hymen. Recommended treatment of the latter is surgical removal, but if the patient has vaginismus, intercourse will still be impossible. The tragedy of this situation is that vaginismus can be treated successfully if the diagnosis is made.

Causes of Vaginismus

Two situations, often coexisting, are prominent in the lives of women with vaginismus. The first is that many are married to impotent men. Whether the men became impotent because they could not have intercourse with their wives or whether the wives developed vaginismus because of their husband's sexual inadequacy is not known. Masters and Johnson point out that if one partner in a marriage is sexually dysfunctional, the other partner probably will become so eventually.

The second prominent factor in the histories of women with vaginismus is a family background in which sexuality is considered sinful, dirty, and totally incompatible with strong religious beliefs. Twelve of the twenty-nine women in Masters and Johnson's series came from this kind of family. Nine of these twelve couples had never been able to have intercourse, although the other three were successful occasionally. Of six men treated at the Foundation who came from restrictive religious families and were primarily impotent, five were married to women who had vaginismus and the same restrictive religious background.

Religious Taboos. The wife whose marriage had been unconsummated for fourteen years came from a family whose attitudes about all physical things were incredibly negative. All her life she had been rigidly controlled under the strictest discipline. The father made the rules, but they were enforced with complete agreement from the mother. Her four sisters all became nuns and her only brother a priest.

Anything that could be considered remotely sexually stimulating was taboo. For example, this girl was not allowed to look at her breasts while taking a bath because of the possibility that the sight might be sexually suggestive. Discussion of menstruation, intercourse, conception, or contraception was not allowed. She and her fiancé courted without any physical contact whatever except for a few kisses when someone else was present. Her response to any sexual suggestion from her intended husband was "withdrawal and confusion." Finally, she was married without any encouragement or advice from her family about sexual relations. The priest who was her adviser told her that intercourse should be tolerated for the purpose of procreation only. It is perfectly understandable that this girl grew up feeling that sexual activity, especially for women, was dirty and debasing.

The husband, who was brought up in the same kind of family, had no resources at all to cope with the wedding-night experience. The resulting trauma was enough to initiate a fourteen-year period of sexual incapacity for the wife. The husband, remarkably, did not become impotent during all those years. He masturbated once in a while, and his wife did it for him once or twice a week. The wife was in psychotherapy when the couple was referred for treatment to the Foundation.

Impotence. Another couple whose religious background was the predominating cause of their difficulties came to the Foundation because the husband had become impotent. He had been able to have intercourse with three different women before being married. But his fiancée came from a very controlling religious family with the result that numerous restrictions were placed by her on their relationship during the engagement. After the usual tiring and anxiety-provoking wedding activities, the husband, knowing that he had been successful before, and completely frustrated by the restrictive courtship, tried to penetrate as soon as he had an erection. His wife, physically and emotionally unprepared, was hurt. She screamed, and he lost his erection.

The couple made other unsuccessful attempts to have intercourse during the honeymoon. They tried almost daily for several months and then tried two or three times a week during the first year of marriage. After a year and a half of marriage, the husband began to lose his ability to have an erection. On the occasions when he had an erection hard enough to penetrate, his hasty attempts hurt his wife and caused her to withdraw even further from physical contact. Finally, the husband had eight months of psychotherapy, but no one thought that the wife might be the source of the problem.

These two couples simply never had the opportunity to develop any emotionally healthy attitudes about sex.

The inhibitions of their parents about physical things were rigidly reinforced by the apparent religious sanction of such taboos. When parents create a taboo and call God to enforce it, the effect, as might be expected, is overwhelming.

Physical Assault. Masters and Johnson report that the long-term emotional effects of a physical attack on a woman may cause vaginismus.

One young woman who had previously been completely sexually functional was a victim of a gang rape. The attack was so brutal that she spent two weeks in the hospital and required extensive surgical reconstruction and repair of her vagina. None of the physicians who took care of her at the time talked with her about the possible emotional effects of the experience or suggested to her that she might need some psychotherapeutic support.

She met her husband-to-be a year after the attack, and they married the following year. Before marriage, the husband was informed in detail about the rape and the injuries. Even though he was sexually experienced and was truly responsive to his wife's need for kindness and gentleness, this couple was unable to have intercourse. They were referred to the Foundation after three years of marriage, and the wife was shown to have severe vaginismus.

Two other women with vaginismus as a result of psychosexual trauma were treated at the Foundation. Their histories were almost identical. As young girls, aged fifteen and seventeen, they had been forced, one by an older brother and the other by her father, into sexual activities with strangers. These youngsters were hurt, exploited, and sometimes punished. When they were able to leave their families, they steered clear of all sexual relations until they finally married at ages twenty-five and twenty-nine. Neither could have intercourse; both had severe vaginismus. Neither of the husbands knew about his wife's experiences, but when they were told, both were extremely cooperative with the therapy program.

Painful Intercourse. Masters and Johnson treated five women who developed vaginismus after long toleration of painful intercourse. The unfortunate feature of these cases is that there was something physically wrong with these women, but doctors had told them that their illness was mental.

Two of these patients had tears of the broad ligaments which support the uterus. (See Chapter 15, Painful Intercourse.) One had had her legs held together by nurses during hard labor so that the obstetrician would be present at the delivery. (Incredible as it sounds, this is not an infrequent procedure.) The first time she and her husband had intercourse after the baby was born, the woman had pain with deep thrusting. The pain increased with every sexual experience, and the wife tried to avoid sexual contact, decreasing it from two or three times a week to two or three times a month. When a physician told the patient that there was nothing physically wrong, the husband demanded intercourse more frequently. The wife refused, and the couple separated for ten months. During that time, the wife tried to have sexual relations with two other men, but the pain caused by deep thrusting of the penis was so severe that she could not continue either relationship. The couple was reunited by a clergyman, but at that time they found penetration impossible because of vaginismus, and after eight months they were referred for therapy. The injuries causing the pain were diagnosed by physical examination at the Foundation, and the woman was referred for surgical correction of the ligamental tears. The couple later returned to the Foundation for treatment of the vaginismus.

Two other women who developed vaginismus after painful intercourse had pelvic endometriosis, a condition in which the endometrium (lining of the uterus) grows in other areas of the pelvis. One of these women had been married eight years before being referred to the Foundation for treatment. The couple had been able to have intercourse once or twice during the first two years of marriage but never thereafter. The wife had actually moaned and screamed every time the husband thrust deeply in the vagina. This couple had had intensive psychotherapy, the wife for four years and the husband for three, before their referral. The pelvic disease and vaginismus were diagnosed at the Foundation. After surgical correction of the endometriosis, the couple returned to St. Louis for treatment of vaginismus.

The fifth woman in whom vaginismus developed after painful intercourse was a widow of sixty-two who had not had sexual relations for ten years. At the age of sixty-one she married a man of sixty-four. The couple could not have intercourse without causing the woman great distress, and this pain occurred even though the husband penetrated only part way. With embarrassment and reluctance the woman consulted her doctor, who gave her some replacement hormones to make the vaginal walls more distensible. After the treatment and six weeks of continence, the husband still was unable to penetrate even though the vaginal walls showed the full effect of the hormone therapy. This woman had developed vaginismus because of the painful intercourse and because she was embarrassed and reluctant to admit to sexual activity at her age. A large part of her treatment consisted of reassurance that sexual activity at sixty-two is normal and desirable.

Homosexual Orientation. Masters and Johnson treated two homosexual women with vaginismus. One of these was a young woman who had been an active homosexual since her seduction by an older sister at age twelve. She married her husband because he was a successful professional man who could give her social status and security, but they could not consummate the marriage for eighteen months. Once involved in the treatment program, however, with the husband fully informed about the problem, this woman became heterosexually functional. She was able to have orgasm during intercourse two weeks after the therapy program ended.

Treatment

Regardless of the cause of vaginismus or the associated problems, treatment can be approached with confidence. If the husband understands that his wife is not malingering, and if both partners share in the treatment, therapy should be highly successful.

According to Masters and Johnson, the most important part of the treatment of vaginismus is to show both husband and wife that the vaginal spasm is real. This removes any doubt in the mind of either partner that there is a well-defined physical problem.

The therapists use illustrations to explain vaginismus in detail, anatomically and physiologically. Then the constriction is physically demonstrated to both partners. The demonstration takes place in an ordinary medical treatment room with the husband present and with the wife lying on an examining table suitably draped and positioned for a pelvic examination. As soon as the examiner attempts to insert a finger into the vaginal canal, the involuntary spasm closes off the outlet. Often the woman herself is more surprised than the husband at the tightness and severity of the constriction. The husband is also asked to put on rubber examining gloves so that he can feel the constriction himself. After this, say Masters and Johnson, "the therapist is dealing with a receptive, if somewhat astonished audience."

From this point on, the treatment of vaginismus is accomplished quite easily, with the physical aspect of it being done by the couple themselves. They are given vaginal dilators in graduated sizes to be used in their own bedroom. At first the husband inserts the dilator with the wife guiding him by hand. Then as her confidence grows and the spasm lessens, larger dilators are introduced by the husband with the wife giving directions. When the wife can accommodate a fairly large dilator, she is encouraged to keep it in place for several hours during the night. If the dilators are used every day, most of the spasm is gone in three to five days, although the dilators may be needed before intercourse during the first four to six weeks after treatment. In many patients, however, the spasm disappears completely after a few days' treatment.

While it is relatively easy to deal with the physical aspect of vaginismus, the emotional aspect must be treated also. There is no question that relief of the physical distress leaves the emotional problems more amenable to treatment. The therapists take this opportunity above all to inform these women of what they can legitimately expect from their sexual lives. Women who have been inhibited by religious sanctions, who are married to impotent men, who have been traumatized by rape or by severely painful intercourse or are otherwise emotionally damaged from whatever cause must be helped to allow themselves a sexual existence.

With their physical problems resolved, with the cooperation of their husbands assured, with confidence in the therapists, and with new knowledge of what to expect from sexual relations, all the women treated for vaginismus by Masters and Johnson became sexually functional. Sixteen of them had orgasm for the first time in their lives during the treatment program. Six who had been able to have orgasm before a specific traumatic episode were again able to reach climax. Four more experienced orgasm during follow-up period after treatment, and only three have not yet been able to have orgasm, although their vaginismus is gone.

CHAPTER 15

Painful Intercourse

Dyspareunia (painful intercourse) is thought of as exclusively a female problem, but men can have this difficulty too. In women the causes range from easily identifiable injuries to obscure psychologic problems. In men painful intercourse is much less frequent, and the cause is likely to be a physical abnormality.

Painful Intercourse in Women

Complaints of painful intercourse are common and often are difficult for physicians to manage. In most instances a physical examination does not reveal the cause. Probably in these cases a combination of psychologic and physiologic events related to the woman's attitudes toward her partner and toward sex is involved.

Some doctors, however, believe they must diagnose a physical problem or state emphatically that nothing is wrong. Even when a careful and extremely thorough physical examination shows no abnormality, Masters and Johnson say it is a mistake to deny authoritatively a woman's persistent complaint of severe pain. For this reason they discuss in detail in their book the possible causes of painful intercourse both physical and psychologic. They advise that in making a diagnosis of the cause of painful intercourse in women the anatomic location, character and timing of the pain during sexual activity are all important. Following is a brief discussion of the various causes of dyspareunia in relation to where the pain is, how severe it is, and when it occurs.

Pain in the Vagina. One of the most common causes of aching, burning, or itching during intercourse is *failure to lubricate,* which actually indicates failure to be sexually aroused. It cannot be diagnosed by physical examination in the doctor's office because it is a psychophysiologic problem obvious only during sexual activity. Sometimes inadequate lubrication causes pain for the male partner too. *The production of lubricating material in the vagina is the response parallel to erection in a man; without it a woman is not ready either physiologically or psychologically for intercourse.* Failure to develop adequate vaginal lubrication happens most commonly, as one might guess, when the woman has no affection, respect, personal identification with, or understanding for her partner, or when she feels none of these things from him. Masters and Johnson point out that burning, aching, and itching are not the kinds of pain women imagine or contrive to avoid intercourse. Women who are using pain as an excuse usually describe it as a "hurting" deep in the vagina during thrusting.

Various fears are another common cause of inadequate lubrication. If a woman fears pregnancy, pain, sexual inadequacy in the man, or social retribution, her natural responses will be inhibited. The same will be true if she thinks sex is dirty or depraved and has never allowed herself to think or react sexually; these women can be helped with information and psychotherapy. Sometimes a woman in any of these situations will lubricate enough for entry but then stop lubricating when thrusting begins.

Many women do not lubricate adequately simply because of the aging process; they can, of course, be treated with replacement hormones.

Frequently, homosexual women will not lubricate well during heterosexual activity, although they are completely adequate with other females. These women are not amenable to treatment because they have no real interest in a male partner.

Infection is the next most common cause of burning, itching, and aching in the vagina. The vagina produces a natural protection against infection because its secretions are normally acid. This normal acidity must be greatly reduced before infectious agents can grow. The natural vaginal protection is lessened during menstruation because the menstrual blood, especially if retained by a tampon, neutralizes the normal acidity.

One of the most widely held misconceptions about feminine hygiene is that routine douching is necessary after intercourse. Masters and Johnson say that nothing could be further from the truth. The vagina returns to its normally protective acid condition within a few hours after intercourse. Douching does no more than remove the residual acid and make the vagina vulnerable to bacterial or fungal growth. Doctors should reassure women that all they need to do is to wash their external genitals with soap and water if they wish to remove whatever seminal fluid or vaginal secretions are outside the vaginal canal.

The sources of vaginal infection are generally intercourse or contamination from the rectum, hands, clothing, or a foreign substance pushed into the vagina. The most common vaginal infections are caused by bacteria, but two other kinds of infections, trichomonal (caused by a protozoan) and monilial (by a fungus), also occur frequently. Painful intercourse caused by infection can be eliminated by proper diagnosis and treatment.

Of *bacterial* invaders in the vagina, the most common come from the colon and rectum. A persistent infection with these kinds of bacteria suggests that the couple is using a technique of rectal intercourse in which the man inserts his penis in the woman's rectum, thrusts there through the plateau phase and then, at the stage of inevitability, withdraws from the rectum and inserts his penis in the vagina to ejaculate. The penis, of course, has been contaminated with the bacteria that are always present in the rectum, and these organisms are introduced into the vagina.

Masters and Johnson suggest to physicians that any patient who has repeated vaginal infections with colonic bacteria be asked if she is having rectal intercourse. If she says she is not, out of embarrassment or whatever, they recommend that the physician do a rectal examination, allowing his gloved finger to remain in the rectum for a few seconds. If the woman has been having rectal intercourse fairly regularly, the rectum usually will relax involuntarily. The response of a person who has not been having rectal intercourse is usually one of rectal spasm which continues throughout the examination. Relaxation of the rectum is not a sure diagnostic sign, but it helps the physician to discuss the situation with a little more assurance. The main point of trying to find out whether or not the woman is having rectal intercourse is to prevent chronic, resistant infections. The physician must emphasize to the couple that the man should ejaculate in the rectum if he penetrates there first.

A *trichomonal* infection in the vagina produces cream colored or bloody discharge, pain and burning. It can be diagnosed by physical examination of the vagina and confirmed by examination of the discharge with a microscope. If the wife has the infection repeatedly, the husband should be treated simultaneously because he can carry the trichomonads too.

Monilial infections of the vagina can cause swelling and weeping of the soft tissues as well as intense burning and itching. They can cause severe pain during intercourse and while urinating. Sometimes diabetic women and women who are being treated with antibotics for an infection elsewhere in the body get monilial vaginitis.

Vaginal *sensitivity* to many substances can cause continual painful intercourse. The main treatment of sensitivity reactions is to discover and eliminate the offending substance. Chemical contraceptive substances are among the most common offenders, and a few women are even sensitive to the rubber in diaphragms and condoms. When there is itching and burning but no infection, sensitivity to one of these substances is a possibility. The potentially harmful effect of frequent douching was mentioned with regard to infections. In addition to disrupting the protective acid environment of the vagina, frequent douching may cause some women to develop sensitivity reactions to the products used in the douching solution. Masters and Johnson say unequivocally that routine douching after intercourse is totally unnecessary.

A frequent cause of painful burning and irritation of the vagina in the fifty-to-seventy age group is *thinning of the vaginal walls* as hormone production lessens; this is called senile vaginitis. These thin walls crack, become irritated and bleed easily during intercourse, causing discomfort which can last hours or even days. These women can be treated very effectively with replacement of sex hormones.

Pain in the Vaginal Outlet and Clitoris. When penetration is painful, Masters and Johnson recommend that a very careful examination be made of the opening of the vagina and the area around it including the clitoris. If the hymen is still intact or if injured parts of it are still present, this is an obvious source of irritation. Pain can be caused by a scar resulting from a tear during the birth of a child, criminal abortion, or rape. An enlargement of the small glands in the inner lips of the vagina can also cause pain during entry, and in postmenopausal women the vaginal outlet may have lost so much of its distensibility that pain on entry is inevitable.

The clitoris is another possible source of pain during penetration. It should be examined very carefully because many women are too embarrassed to tell or show a doctor exactly where the pain is. Sometimes material collected under the foreskin of the clitoris irritates the area; intense burning results as the man tries to penetrate the vagina. If irritation is present, any movement of the clitoral foreskin during foreplay or entry may be painful. Even if there is no irritation, the male partner can cause pain if he tries to stimulate the clitoral glans (head of the clitoris) during the beginning of foreplay as many marriage manuals recommend. Chapter 13 on orgasmic dysfunction explains why this usually is not stimulating. The sensitized clitoris can be very painful as the man tries to insert his penis.

All the problems involving pain in the vaginal outlet

can be solved, some by surgical correction, others obviously by education and improved coital technique.

Pain Deep in the Pelvis. It is often difficult to sort out the problems of women who complain of severe pain deep in the pelvis. Many of them are avoiding unwelcome sexual activity by complaining of pain, but a few have serious physical problems.

Masters and Johnson treated eleven patients who had *lacerations (tears) in the ligaments which support the uterus.* Five of these tears were caused during childbirth, three by criminal abortion, and three by gang rape. All these women needed surgical repair of their injuries, not psychotherapy. A prominent finding during the physical examination of these women is a uterus which is tipped back. The cervix (opening of the uterus) can be moved in any direction without corresponding movement of the body of the uterus itself. It gives the doctor the impression that the cervix and body of the uterus are not really attached. Any movement of the cervix, especially upward, causes pain, to which the patient usually says, "It's just like the pain I have with intercourse."

The women whose injuries were caused by obstetrical trauma or criminal abortion were able to tell that the pain definitely began after a particular obstetrical experience. They describe the pain during thrusting as if the husband had "hit something" with his penis. Other complaints related to increased pelvic congestion are also associated, such as backache, throbbing in the pelvis, a tired feeling, painful menstruation, and sometimes a feeling that "everything is falling out." If a woman has to stand for a long time during her daily activities, these symptoms intensify.

The three victims of gang rape were assaulted not

only many times, but also were entered vaginally and rectally at the same time and had foreign objects jammed into the vagina. Many tears in the vagina, bladder, and rectum were repaired at the time of the injury, but injuries to the ligaments supporting the uterus had never been diagnosed. Doctors had assumed that the complaints of painful intercourse were psychologically related to the trauma of rape.

After surgery for repair of their uterine ligament lacerations, the symptoms of painful intercourse, painful menstruation, and fatigue were totally relieved in some women and almost completely relieved in others. Masters and Johnson describe this syndrome and the surgical findings in some detail in their book, with the hope of making the physician increasingly aware of this problem.

Two other causes of pain felt deep in the pelvis on thrusting are *infections in the cervix, uterus and tubes, and endometriosis.* Endometriosis is an abnormal condition in which the tissue that normally lines the uterus implants and grows in other places in the pelvis. The infections can be caused by venereal disease, especially gonorrhea, or by organisms that are normally found on the skin and in the colon.

Although endometriosis and infectious disease are two completely separate conditions, both produce pain deep in the pelvis in essentially the same way. Irritation of the pelvic organs causes fibrous tissue to grow between them. Instead of being soft and freely movable, the tissues become hard and inelastic. The increase in vaginal size which occurs with sexual excitement and the movement during thrusting put tension on these rigid tissues, causing pain.

A woman who has had a *hysterectomy* will sometimes

have painful intercourse afterward. Masters and Johnson cite three major causes of pain after this operation: the stitches may have been placed so that the penis hits the resulting scar; a woman whose ovaries as well as uterus were removed may not have been given replacement hormones which would keep the pelvic tissues soft, and a woman who has not been properly reassured may feel that she is less of a woman since she can no longer have children. It is especially important for any woman who must have a hysterectomy to be reassured that her sexual drive and ability to have orgasms will not be affected. She should, in fact, feel better after the corrective operation, lose any unconscious fears of an unwanted pregnancy, and have more sexual interest than before.

Infection, endometriosis, tears of the uterine supports, and postsurgical complications are not the only causes of deep pelvic pain during intercourse. Tumors and ovarian cysts can cause pain, but these are easily diagnosed and therefore rarely overlooked by physicians.

The diagnosis of psychosomatic pain can be made only by carefully eliminating all other possible causes, Dr. Masters stresses. He states unequivocally that the physician who labels pain during intercourse as psychosomatic, without taking a pertinent history and performing a very careful pelvic examination, is risking mismanagement of his patient.

Painful Intercourse in Men

Pain during or after intercourse can be so incapacitating for a man that he cannot enjoy sexual relations. Many of these problems are treatable, but they have been neglected in the medical literature, says Masters.

The penile glans (head of the penis) becomes so exquisitely tender in many men right after ejaculation that they cannot keep it in the vagina. Men with this abnormal *sensitivity of the glans* learn to withdraw immediately after ejaculating. Sometimes the pain is not so severe as at other times, but since the man has no way of knowing beforehand what will happen after he has orgasm, he withdraws. Men who are not circumcised can get relief occasionally by pulling the foreskin well back over the head of the penis.

Another cause of painful intercourse in men is *poor hygiene*. If a man is not circumcised, the foreskin must be pulled back and the head of the penis and undersurface of the foreskin washed with soap and water routinely. When this is not done periodically, material which collects under the foreskin will cause inflammation and irritation, especially if it becomes infected. Thrusting or even just entry can be painful.

Some men have such a small opening of the foreskin that it cannot be pulled back over the head of the penis. This condition is called *phimosis*. Irritation and infection are bound to occur in this situation. In addition, fibrous tissue forms between the foreskin and the glans so that the foreskin can no longer be moved. This produces a lot of pressure on the glans with every erection, and it can be extremely painful. The only treatment is circumcision.

Foundation therapists have also treated a few men who had a true hypersensitivity of the glans. Anything that touched it, including clothing or body contact, was irritating. One man was hypersensitive to the environment of the vagina. Even though he had intercourse with many different women, the reaction afterward was always the same—blistering and peeling of the head of the penis. His problem was solved by giving him something with which to coat the glans before entry.

Hypersensitivity reactions of the penis caused by the vaginal environment and allergic reactions to contraceptive creams, jellies, foams, and douching preparations may cause inflammation and blistering of the penis. If the blisters break, intercourse can be extremely painful for the man. The treatment, of course, is a change in contraceptive method, change of douche preparation, or elimination of douching entirely.

Infections in the vaginal canal can also cause local infection of the penis. Burning and itching after intercourse result, just as in women. Gonorrhea particularly can cause severe pain during and right after ejaculation. The inflammatory process caused by the infection results in narrowing of the urethra (the channel leading through the penis from the urinary bladder). This narrowing makes both urination and ejaculation painful. Treatment of gonorrheal infection is more effective if begun immediately after exposure rather than waiting weeks or months.

Masters and Johnson mention in their book a few unusual conditions which cause pain in either the glans or shaft of the penis. Among these is *downward bowing of the erect penis* caused by trauma. Of the four men they saw with this condition, two had been hit sharply on the erect penis by angry women. Each of the other two had been having intercourse with his partner in the superior position when his penis slipped out of the vagina. In both cases the woman tried to get it back in by sitting down quickly on the penis. In her haste she missed the vaginal opening and sat down with full weight on the erect penis. Each of the four men, in describing his painful and disastrous experience said, "I felt (or I heard) something snap." Bleeding into the tissues was followed gradually by scarring with a slowly developing downward bowing of the penis. So far surgical correction of this problem has provided relatively poor results. Sometimes the operation makes it worse. Both masturbation and intercourse are painful for these men.

Spasm of the prostate gland in older men, inflammation of the prostate gland (often caused by too much alcohol), enlargement of the prostate that comes with aging, and rarely cancer of the prostate may also cause pain during ejaculation, although these conditions are rare.

CHAPTER 16

Sex in the Aging

The sexual revolution among today's youth is less radical than the new information Masters and Johnson have published about the sexual responses of the aging. What they have learned will be relevant to the lives of millions of people in the fifty-to-seventy age group, especially men. The middle-aged man worries about becoming a sexual has-been. As soon as he notices the normal changes in his sexual response pattern that come with aging, he worries about them. His masculinity is at stake. These fears are unnecessary, according to Masters and Johnson. A man in good health, who has a partner in whom he is interested and who is interested in him, should enjoy an active sex life even in his eighties.

Ignorance is one of the greatest deterrents to effective sexual functioning at all ages, but it has been most damaging to the aging. Myths about sex patterns in this group have been perpetuated simply because the facts were unknown. Not until Masters and Johnson reported their findings has any accurate information on this subject been available.

In *Human Sexual Inadequacy* the authors tell about a typical couple in their early sixties who came for treatment. Through many years of marriage this couple had always enjoyed sex, until the husband noticed that getting an erection took longer than usual. After this happened a few times his concern intensified to fright, and he became impotent. A few months later when the couple consulted a doctor, he told them that the husband's condition was a natural result of aging, that men lose their ability to have an erection and that they should learn to accept this since nothing can be done to correct it.

For five years this couple lived unhappily with the husband's impotence. During that time they consulted several other doctors who gave them the same advice as the first, until finally one physician referred them to the Foundation for therapy, where they again became sexually functional. How did Masters and Johnson manage it?

The Aging Male

The research studies in sexual physiology in the Foundation's laboratory included observations of sexual functioning both in young men and in older men. In human males, regardless of their age, there were four stages to the sexual response cycle: the *excitement* phase (getting an erection), the *plateau* phase (increasing sexual tensions, thus maintaining the erection), the *orgasmic* phase (ejaculation), and finally, the *resolution* phase (return of the penis to its flaccid or soft condition). Masters and Johnson found that these four stages change as men get older. If the middle-aged man and his wife are aware of these changes and take them into account during their lovemaking, there is no reason why pleasurable sex cannot continue. The reason the response cycle changes is that body processes slow down with age, *but they do not stop*. In the treatment of aging couples, Foundation therapists explain these changes and tell the patients how to modify their sexual behavior accordingly.

The excitement phase usually takes more time for a middle-aged man. It takes longer to get an erection, and the erection may not be as hard initially as when he was younger. Men who first experience this slowdown often panic because our society has conditioned every male to expect this sign as the beginning of the end of sexual pleasures and the conscious recognition that old age has arrived. As Dr. Masters puts it, "an aging male does achieve an erection at a slower rate, but he also can't run around the block as fast. As he notices his erective slowdown he usually thinks, 'Oh God, it's gone and there is nothing I can do about it.' And so he worries and doesn't have an erection. But the loss of erection is only secondary. His potential for erection remains unchanged. Can you think of the effect this will have if we can just get this concept across?"

During the plateau phase the man over fifty has a lot of advantages over his younger counterpart. His ejaculatory control is much greater. He can maintain an erection for a long time after he reaches a completely pleasurable level of sexual tension without experiencing the strong drive to ejaculate with which a younger man must contend. Those men who have a pre-ejaculatory secretion in the plateau phase find that the amount of secretion lessens with age. This is normal. It does not affect sexual functioning.

Most changes in the aging male's response pattern happen in the ejaculatory phase. Ejaculation usually happens in two stages. The first is the "inevitability stage," that period when the man feels he is going to ejaculate, when he can no longer hold back; the second is the "expulsion stage" when the seminal fluid is expelled from the penis. After fifty years of age the inevitability stage may be shortened (two to four seconds instead of four to seven seconds), or it may not occur at all. A one-stage ejaculation is very common in this group. It may be caused by "hormone deprivation," a decreased amount of the male sex hormone, testosterone. Frequently it happens when a man delays ejaculation for a long time, usually holding off for his partner to have orgasm.

Some men who have problems related to lowered hormone production can be treated by the administration of testosterone, although Masters and Johnson emphasize that little is known now about hormone replacement in men. They have also observed that expulsion of the semen is less forceful in older men and that there is not as much seminal fluid as in younger men. These changes progress with aging, but an older man, as long as he realizes that he will not lose his erective ability with age, enjoys sexual activity.

An older man may lose his erection within seconds after ejaculating, his resolution phase being much shorter than that of a younger man. In addition, he may have a longer refractory phase—he may not be able to have another erection for many hours, while a younger man, with effective stimulation, might be able to have another erection within minutes.

Masters and Johnson explain to older people that they must allow nature a little more time to take her course. If a man stops trying to will an erection, but just lets it happen naturally, he will continue to be potent. Instructions given to aging couples also include techniques of stimulating foreplay (p. 144 and pp. 175–180). The wife is made to understand that she should not interpret the slower responses of her husband as evidence that he does not find her attractive anymore. Instead, both are encouraged by the therapists to learn to enjoy the longer period of foreplay. In addition, the wife can learn the skill of inserting the penis when it is not fully erect, knowing that the first few thrusts will add the necessary stimulation to get full erection.

Because of lessened ejaculatory demand and better ejaculatory control, a man, often for the first time in his life, finds it easy to satisfy a wife whose responses were always slower than his. The wife now has the opportunity to feel sexual in a way that she never had before. The husband really has become a better lover.

The most important change for older couples to be aware of, however, is that as he ages the older man definitely has less *need* to ejaculate. Masters and Johnson state:

> *This factor of reduced ejaculatory demand for the aging male is the entire basis for effective prolongation of sexual functioning in the aging population.*[1]

If an older man ejaculates only when he really needs to, he will retain his erective ability and can continue to have intercourse regularly. This is an important new concept for both men and women. The stereotyped attitude about intercourse is that both partners feel ineffective if the man does not ejaculate. Sex needs vary from person to person, and should be met according

---

[1] *HSI*, p. 323.

to the individual's need, but at no time is this principle more important than when the partners are over fifty. If the husband and wife do not understand this, they may force ejaculation even when the man does not feel the demand for it, and as a result the aging man's erective powers will diminish. "If someone asked me what the single most important statement is in *Human Sexual Inadequacy,* I would pick this material on the aging male," says Dr. Masters. "It is going to affect more people directly than any one thing if we can just get it disseminated. This sense of worth will create productivity in all areas of daily living—including in bed."

The Aging Female

The prevailing attitudes about the sex life of the older woman are among the most destructive traditions in our culture. Almost nowhere does more inaccurate information exist. Many women believe that it is unnatural for them to continue sexual relations. Their mothers may have told them, as their grandmothers before, that a woman's sex life should end once her children grow up and she reaches menopause. These women look forward to the time when they will no longer be expected to submit to a "dirty or bothersome act," in which a dutiful wife is expected to participate but not enjoy. Masters and Johnson's observations of older couples in their laboratory and their clinical experience in the treatment program show that it is completely normal and certainly beneficial for older women to continue sexual activity. They explain for their women patients, just as they do for the men, what changes aging brings and how to cope with them.

Women experience the same slowing process and the same hormone deprivation with aging that men do. As a result there are changes in the sexual response cycle and in the anatomy of the sex organs. These changes need not cause any woman to be sexually dysfunctional, but the slowing process must be understood and accepted and the hormone problem treated if necessary.

The four phases of the female sexual response cycle are analogous to those in the male—excitement, plateau, orgasmic, and resolution. Vaginal lubrication, the first sign of sexual excitement in the female, occurs more slowly with aging, and less lubricant is produced. Younger women take fifteen to thirty seconds for lubrication, but it may take four or five minutes of sex play to initiate it in older women because the thin and smooth vaginal walls no longer offer a good medium through which to secrete lubrication. The clitoris may get smaller also, but it will still respond to sexual stimulation and transmit sexual excitement.

In the plateau phase of the response cycle there is much less elevation of the uterus and therefore much less increase in the size of the vaginal canal. Older women also do not have the sex skin-color changes which appear in younger women nor the changes in the labia majora (outer lips of the vagina).

Older women usually experience a shorter orgasmic phase, just as men do. If a young woman had eight to twelve vaginal contractions during orgasm, as she gets older she may have only four or five. Only one or two uterine contractions may be identifiable, instead of three to five. Sometimes orgasm will cause a painful spastic contraction of the uterus. This symptom usually means that sex hormone levels are below normal, and it can be relieved by replacement therapy. The resolution phase is rapid, just as in men.

Dr. Masters has been a strong proponent of using hormone replacement therapy to treat the hot flashes, irritability and nervousness that plague many menopausal women. After menopause, intercourse may be painful for women because hormone deprivation causes the vaginal walls to become thin and less distensible so that they crack and bleed easily. Treatment with replacement hormones will partly restore the vaginal wall to its functional state, relieving this problem.

The responses of aging women vary. Some never need hormone replacement therapy in order to remain sexually responsive. Their hormone production lessens, but they continue to produce lubricant in adequate amounts. These women seem to breeze through menopause without difficulty, and they retain effective sexual functioning through the years. Others show the physical signs of aging with markedly lowered hormone levels but do not suffer spastic contractions of the uterus, nor do they have problems of maintaining sufficient vaginal lubrication or having painful intercourse. These women continue to respond well because they have had sexual intercourse once or twice a week over the years. The psychologic and physical advantages that come through the release of sexual tensions on a regular basis seem to help overcome the effects of hormone starvation.

Masters and Johnson have also found from their studies that there is an increase in the rate of masturbation in older women. This is understandable since many have become widowed, divorced, or isolated from male sex partners. Husbands may be ill and thus not participating in sex. There is no reason why these women who still need release from sexual tension should not provide it for themselves.

Treatment Results

Statistics in *Human Sexual Inadequacy* show that the longer a person has lived with his sexual difficulty the less chance there is for reversal. Older people had a failure rate of thirty percent which is much higher than the rate of failure in younger people.

Of the fifty-six aging couples who were referred for therapy, fifty-one were in treatment because the husband requested it. The male therefore assumes special significance in Masters and Johnson's figures. Thirty-four of the husbands were in their fifties, eighteen were in their sixties, and four were over seventy. Wives of the fifty-six men spanned an age range from twenty-eight to seventy-nine; of these, thirty-seven were over fifty. Only these thirty-seven women were considered in the statistical analysis of treatment of aging people. Fifteen of these women had never had orgasm, twelve occasionally had orgasm, and ten were functioning well sexually. Of the fifty-six aging couples, there were thirty-three instances in which both the wife and husband had a sexual problem; in the rest only one partner was obviously dysfunctional. The older the couples the greater the incidence of two dysfunctional partners. Twenty-eight of the husbands complained that they had become impotent; twenty-three of the wives complained that they had never had orgasm.

Masters and Johnson make a special point of mentioning that it is always worth trying to reverse sexual difficulty in persons over fifty because there is at least a fifty percent chance of success even if the problem has existed for twenty-five years or more. If a therapist can restore effective sexual functioning half of the time, his effort is well spent.

That sexual functioning is normal in older people should be recognized and accepted. They come to maintain their sexual identity while continuing to enjoy the physical and psychologic benefits that result. Our culture has conditioned aging men and women not to expect sex or to enjoy sex, and it is this attitude that Masters and Johnson hope to change.

CHAPTER 17

Doctors and Other Therapists: Do They Always Help?

Until recently most medical schools did not teach courses in sexual function. The need of people in distress and the acceptance of sexuality by the younger generation have forced medical-school faculties to accept the subject as not only honorable but valuable. The first course in human sexual function ever taught at a medical school was offered by Dr. Masters in the department of obstetrics and gynecology at Washington University School of Medicine in St. Louis in 1960. It was a required course for seniors, but one quarter of the class refused to return to the classroom for the second lecture. Student complaints to the dean and the chairman of the department forced the school to make the course elective rather than required. That such a large percentage of senior students felt this material to be too personal and embarrassing for classroom consideration is astounding. These people were to be graduated soon as medical doctors who would be asked to counsel patients with sexual difficulties.

"Several years ago we had to show a psychiatrist patient what the clitoris is because he had no idea," says

Masters. Dr. Harold Lief, who has studied the sex attitudes of medical students extensively reported:

> As late as 1959, a study of medical students from five Philadelphia medical schools revealed that half of them thought—after three or four years in medical school—that masturbation itself is a frequent cause of mental illness. Worse yet, a fifth of the medical school faculty members shared the same misconception.[1]

There has been relatively rapid change in medical-school curricula since 1960. Eighty-eight medical schools now have or are planning courses in sexual function.[2] When one takes into account the changes in attitudes during the last decade, it is difficult to imagine the student reaction Dr. Masters encountered in 1960 happening today. Masters and Johnson provided something medical schools could teach. *Human Sexual Response* is now being used as a textbook of sexual physiology in many schools, and *Human Sexual Inadequacy* will no doubt become its clinical counterpart for courses in sexology. Dr. Masters comments, "I don't think there will be any medical school not teaching courses in sexual function by 1975. And after all, that will be only fifteen years—pretty fast to change the curriculum of all the medical schools in the country."

One cannot blame physicians for not knowing how to deal with problems of sexual inadequacy. "There are very few physicians practicing medicine today," Masters

---

[1] Lief, H. I., "Teaching Doctors about Sex," in Brecher, R., and Brecher, E., *An Analysis of Human Sexual Response* (Boston: Little, Brown, 1966), pp. 276-277.

[2] Lief, H. I., "New Developments in Sex Education of the Physician," *Journal of the American Medical Association*, 212 (June 15, 1970), pp. 1864-1867.

says, "who have ever had a moment's training in human sexual response while they were in medical school. Most of them were out of medical school when this was beginning to be taught in the mid 1960's. The fellows who took the courses then are still in residency now."

Masters and Johnson do not claim to be sex educators, except at a postgraduate level. They see their role as students of sexology and suppliers of basic information which others can shape into programs for various ages and educational levels. Today, as in the past, sex education often means teaching fallacy and superstition, whether it be taught in the home, the school, the church, or the doctor's office. Masters and Johnson feel all four can contribute to sex education if accurate information is available, but one alone cannot do the job well.

Masters says the best home-style sex education is exposure to spontaneous warmth and affection between parents. "There is nothing that teaches about sex half so much as Pop patting Mom's fanny as he walks by her in the kitchen. Obviously she loves it, and the kids watch and say, 'Boy, that's for me.' That's sex education as it can be done in the home. I don't mean that Mom and Pop shouldn't answer questions about the birds and the bees. They should."

Doctors and other therapists, because of what they do not know, have frequently made matters worse for their patients by giving inaccurate information about a sexual problem. Of the 213 couples referred for treatment of secondary impotence, twenty-seven of the men had been told by the professional person consulted that they had better forget about sex; nothing could be done to help them. The power of suggestion from authoritative sources is enormous for these men, and such suggestions added immensely to their problems.

Twenty-one were told there was no way of helping them on their first and only visit to a physician. In eleven cases the physician said nothing could be done because of the aging process. The youngest of these men was forty-two and the average age was fifty-three, hardly old men.

Two more, who consulted clergymen after they had seen a doctor, were told that their impotence was punishment for adultery, and a third was told he was being punished for arranging an abortion for his wife. A fourth was assured by a clergyman that his impotence would disappear if he attended church regularly for one year. It is not difficult to guess what happened. Two years later, after faithful church attendance, the man was still impotent. The six remaining men of the twenty-one had consulted psychologists (four), a marriage counselor, and a lay analyst; they were offered comments such as, "Once a grown man has a homosexual experience, he always ends up impotent," or "Any man masturbating after the age of thirty can expect to become impotent." Erective failure progresses rapidly when one hears, from someone who is supposed to know, that it cannot be cured.

There were also six instances in Masters and Johnson's group of patients in which an authoritative suggestion *definitely caused* symptoms of secondary impotence. For example, a woman with vaginismus consulted her physician, her clergyman, and finally a gynecologist who recommended surgical removal of her hymen, to which she readily agreed. Vaginismus was never diagnosed. After surgery the gynecologist remarked to the husband, "Well, if you can't have intercourse now, the fault is certainly yours." But vaginal spasm still persisted even with the hymen removed. When the man found he still could not penetrate, he did indeed think the fault was his and he became impotent.

In another case a husband and wife were enjoying intercourse approximately once a day. Friends convinced them that this was excessive and that they should consult their doctor about it. The physician told them that ejaculating every day would wear the husband out in no time. The power of suggestion was so strong that the man began having erective failure. He became impotent and remained so for seven years before he consulted someone else.

Masters and Johnson also report in *Human Sexual Inadequacy* a high incidence of seduction by therapists of patients who went for help with their sexual problems. They feel strongly that this behavior is destructive. "Why are they going to bed?" asks Masters. "I am not quarreling about two people going to bed together, but I am quarreling if a therapist does it under the guise of, 'All right, I'll help you with your problem, dear.'" Most frequently the pattern is for a woman to be seduced by a male therapist, since there are more male than female therapists in practice.

But male therapists have seduced other men, and female therapists have seduced patients of both sexes. It might be pleasurable for a person to have orgasm with his doctor, psychologist, or clergyman, but it is not going to help a patient's marriage difficulties. Sexual functioning in marriage, Masters and Johnson emphasize, is closely related to communication between the partners. When a therapist substitutes for the spouse, the marriage is likely to deteriorate.

A classic instance reported by Masters and Johnson of a male therapist who seduced a male patient follows:

> The remaining instance of homosexual identification as a plausible etiological agent in primary impotence was that of a virginal man of 21 years referred to psychotherapy for nervous tension, intermittent periods of depression, and compulsive lack of effective academic progress. The therapist convinced the young man that his unresolved tensions were derived from the natural frustrations of a latent homosexual and introduced him to the physical aspects of mouth-genital functioning in a patient-therapist relationship. This homosexual relationship lasted for 18 months, only to be terminated abruptly when the patient's family no longer could afford the cost of the twice-weekly sessions.[8]

Masters comments, "We have definite histories of gynecologists, internists, urologists and psychiatrists, as well as lawyers, priests, rabbis and ministers of all the Protestant denominations—all seducing patients." But of course, most therapists do not attempt to seduce their patients. Masters and Johnson do not want to condemn physicians and other therapists in any general way. They agree most are well motivated, and they genuinely try to help patients with sexual troubles. Many intelligent clergymen work especially hard to create a therapeutic aura for those who come for advice. Clergymen see more people with sexual dysfunction than marriage counselors, psychologists, or doctors.

Professional people have been the first to recognize the value of the Foundation program and to come for

---

[8] *HSI*, p. 141.

treatment themselves. This open-mindedness and receptiveness on their part is certainly encouraging. It indicates a willingness to accept new solutions for their own problems and to use their newly acquired knowledge for the benefit of others.

Of the 510 couples treated at the Foundation by the end of 1969, one or both partners in eighty-nine of these couples was a physician. Of these, half were psychiatrists. In addition, many men and women in the behavorial sciences were also patients. Professionals have come to the Foundation in increasing numbers since *Human Sexual Response* was published in 1966. These people understand the significance of Masters and Johnson's work, and in fact, many psychiatrist patients are adapting Foundation techniques to their own practices.

Psychiatrists have been the source of more patient referrals than any other medical specialty. Perhaps because they appreciate emotional suffering and its frequent sexual component more than other physicians, and because they understand the effects of cultural pressures on people, they were the first to see the advantages of treatment at the Foundation. Masters and Johnson do not look upon themselves as being in competition with psychiatry. Their rapid-treatment method is different from conventional psychiatric treatment. They make no pretense whatever of being able to treat psychoses, personality disorders, or in fact any kind of major psychiatric problem. They direct their efforts to correction of sexual dysfunction and improvement of marriage relationships.

Patients who come to the average doctor with a sex problem have little chance of being treated successfully. Many physicians and others who offer counsel are very poorly prepared to give advice about sexual matters. Unfortunately, they are representative of the general population when it comes to ignorance and bias about sex. Many doctors come from families that have not encouraged healthy sexual attitudes. As Mrs. Johnson says, "Doctors are people first and doctors second. They have all the hangups that the rest of the population has, and are not necessarily more informed or more open about things than anyone else in the general population."

Human Sexual Response has served to enlighten professionals about sex physiology and now *Human Sexual Inadequacy* provides information about treatment of sexual problems. It is most important that professionals lead the way in dispelling the untruths that have persisted in sexology. If professionals do not lead the way, the public may very well force them to learn more about sex. People will not be satisfied with platitudes when they know that help is available at last.

CHAPTER 18

Statistics of the Treatment Program

Masters and Johnson present in their book a detailed statistical analysis of their successes and failures in treatment. Many of these numbers appear in the chapters on the various sexual dysfunctions. Here, in summary form, are some additional facts about the treatment program.

- *Human Sexual Inadequacy* reports a study of 510 married couples and 57 single people.
- Clinical treatment for dysfunction was begun at the Reproductive Biology Research Foundation at the start of 1959. The study continued for eleven years, until the end of 1969.
- Of the 510 couples in the study, 287 had only one dysfunctional partner. Of these, 171 were men, and 116 were women.
- The remaining 223 of the 510 couples had two dysfunctional partners.
- The total number of individuals treated for sexual dysfunction can be classified as follows:

One marriage partner dysfunctional	287
223 marriages with two dysfunctional partners	446
Single men (41 with partner surrogates and 13 with replacement partners)	54
Single women (with replacement partners)	3
Total dysfunctional individuals treated	790

- The youngest person treated was a woman twenty-three years of age, and the oldest was a man of seventy-six.
- In the year 1969, 114 couples and 9 single people were treated at the Foundation.
- There are 6 to 8 couples in therapy at a time.
- The patient population was not representative of the general population because the patients had higher than average income and education and because all were highly motivated. There was also an extremely high percentage of doctors and behavioral scientists in the group. Of the 510 couples treated, there were 89 physician marriages. Of the 790 individuals treated, 413 (52.3 percent) had previous psychotherapy. The fact that couples made the effort to visit St. Louis for therapy indicates that they wanted treatment very much and therefore were more likely to succeed in therapy than randomly selected people.
- Of the 790 individuals treated, 142 were treatment failures at the end of the two-week program, for an initial failure rate of 18.0 percent. Table 1 shows the breakdown of treatment failures for each dysfunction.
- If a patient became permanently dysfunctional at any time during the five-year follow-up, treatment was considered a failure and reported as such in Masters and Johnson's statistics. Overall failure statistics are,

Table 1. *Initial Treatment Failures**

Complaint	Number of Patients	Number of Failures	Initial Failure Rate in Percent
Primary impotence	32	13	40.6
Secondary impotence	213	56	26.2
Premature ejaculation	186	4	2.2
Ejaculatory incompetence	17	3	17.6
Male totals	448	76	16.9
Primary orgasmic dysfunction	193	32	16.6
Situational orgasmic dysfunction	149	34	22.8
Female totals	342	66	19.3
Male and female totals	790	142	18.0

therefore, a combination of initial treatment failures and late failures.

- Of the 313 married and single patients treated from 1959 through 1964, 226 individuals were interviewed five years after their therapy. *This is the first time the long-term results of psychotherapeutic treatment for sexual dysfunction have been reported.*
- Of the 87 patients not interviewed, 56 were initial treatment failures. (Masters and Johnson felt that it might be harmful for these patients to be involved in follow-up proceedings.) The other 31 patients were initially treatment successes, but lost contact with the Foundation and thus were lost to follow-up.
- Subtracting the 31 patients lost to follow-up from the 313 patients treated, leaves 282 patients to be considered in calculating the overall failure rate.

---

* From *HSI*, p. 367.

Seventy-two of these 282 were treatment failures, 56 (19.8 percent) during therapy, and 16 (5.7 percent) during the five-year follow-up, giving an overall failure rate of 25.5 percent *after five years*.
- Conversely, the overall success rate was 74.5 percent *after five years*. This success rate has never been approached by other forms of therapy.
- The difference between the failure rates in men and those in women was not statistically significant.
- Failure rates in the population over 50 years of age were higher than for younger people. The initial failure rate for men over 50 was 25 percent. The initial failure rate of 40.7 percent for women over 50 was at least 50 percent greater than that for younger women.

Comments on Treatment Failures

- The reasons for failure can vary widely, from poor patient motivation to errors in judgment by the cotherapists. Occasionally the Foundation has inadvertently accepted couples for therapy when one partner obviously was not interested in making therapy work and preserving the marriage. Failure has also resulted when the cotherapists failed to relate treatment to the patient's own life style, or when the cotherapists allowed themselves to be misled by an apparent rapid physical cure without in-depth treatment of the marital relationship.
- Acute anxiety in some people was so incapacitating that it was impossible for them to respond in a two-week treatment period.
- Failure to progress in treatment was caused a few

times by partners who withheld information, perhaps relating to incest, homosexuality, rape, or adultery because they believed it to be too devastating or unacceptable to their mates.

- Therapy also has occasionally been sidetracked by what Masters and Johnson call "therapeutic malpractice." Some patients being treated by psychotherapists at home are "coached" by them during therapy at the Foundation, their advice often contradicting Masters and Johnson's instructions. This interference has resulted in a few treatment failures.
- The 31 initially successful patients who were subsequently lost to follow-up remain a statistical enigma. If all eventually became dysfunctional, Masters and Johnson's overall failure rate would be 32.9 percent (103 failures in 313 individuals). On the other hand, if all 31 are still sexually functional (41 failures in 313 individuals), the overall failure rate would be only 13.1 percent.
- Another point about treatment failures that Masters and Johnson themselves have never emphasized is that some patients, who were not successful during the two-week treatment program, became sexually functional a short time after returning home. These people have been categorized as treatment failures because Masters and Johnson wished to present their statistics in the most critical way possible.

PART III

EPILOGUE

EPILOGUE: An interview with Dr. Masters and Mrs. Johnson about their present and future work

MR. BELLIVEAU: After publication of *Human Sexual Response* you went on two extended lecture tours. Now that *Human Sexual Inadequacy* is published are you accepting any of the many lecture offers you receive?

DR. MASTERS: We are receiving fifteen to twenty offers a week to speak, but we rarely accept them. There is an entirely different atmosphere now. We have lectured a lot about sexual facts and fallacies, and we have talked about therapy. There is really no need to talk about therapy now that *Human Sexual Inadequacy* is published. The book can speak for itself. Homosexuality is our next subject, but we are not ready to talk about it yet because we don't yet have anything conclusive to say.

MR. BELLIVEAU: Aren't there a lot of people lecturing on sexual functioning who have not done original work?

DR. MASTERS: No one really comprehends sexual function, but today everyone seems delighted to talk about it on the lecture platform. Today's original thinkers in this field are not talking so much. They are at home working. Our own plans are to stay home and give other professionals something to lecture about.

MRS. RICHTER: Have you already started your research on homosexuality?

DR. MASTERS: Yes, we plan to publish our findings in the mid 1970's. That will mean that we will have worked a decade on this problem. We wouldn't feel secure unless we worked on any problem for that period of time. About seventy-five percent of our study group so far is oriented to the female homosexual.

MRS. RICHTER: Are you following the same plan as previously — laboratory investigation then clinical application?

DR. MASTERS: Yes, we've completed all the work on the physiology of homosexuality; now we are working on homosexual dysfunction. We have male and female patients who would like to become sexually effective heterosexually, and male couples and female couples who are content with their partner choice but are not able to function effectively. For example, we might have a Lesbian couple, and one partner or both is nonorgasmic. Patients make their own partner choices. It is not our role to impose judgments.

MR. BELLIVEAU: How about your future work?

DR. MASTERS: We will continue to follow the formal, basic medical approach to a problem: first, to go to the laboratory; second, to apply from the laboratory to clinical medicine what we have found that is applicable to treatment; and third, to do something about prevention. That is what we are going to do for the next decade. We're planning to work on the prevention of sexual dysfunction.

MR. BELLIVEAU: How are you going to do that?

DR. MASTERS: Last spring we started to study sexually traumatized adolescents. By comparing the onset of trauma in the young with sexually dysfunctional older people, who had some of the same problems when they were young, we ought to learn something in the next decade about causes of sexual dysfunction. If we know the causes of something we should be able to prevent it from happening. Incidentally, we see adolescents only with their parents because it is important that the parents be involved. We hope in 1980 to publish our findings in the field of prevention. We will then have had ten years of experience on that subject.

MRS. RICHTER: You've been working on postmarital counseling as a preventive measure?

MRS. JOHNSON: Yes, we have. Premarital counseling usually means a discussion of contraception; this is not really premarital counseling. If we can be available to couples *after* their marriage, when they know what their problems are, then with short-term help they can perhaps be completely functional sexually. This is the time to counsel. If they still have a new relationship and we can take care of their minor physical and psychosocial problems, they are unlikely to have future troubles, at least not of the same order. We are seeing these couples in group discussions.

MR. BELLIVEAU: Is the average reader capable of helping himself after reading *Human Sexual Inadequacy?*

MRS. JOHNSON: The quality of the relationship between the reader and his partner would be the most important factor in the answer to that question. So would, of course, the ability to comprehend the material.

DR. MASTERS: Yes, a lot has to do with the marital relationship. Could a man learn ejaculatory control if he practiced the squeeze technique effectively? Yes, he could do that, but the real question is whether or not he is really able to deal with the problems involved in the marital relationship. The physical part can usually be corrected easily.

MRS. JOHNSON: The physical dysfunction is often on the surface; usually there are many other problems to be worked on, especially if the dysfunction has existed for a long time.

DR. MASTERS: With the squeeze technique someone could learn ejaculatory control if he had a partner who could really cooperate. If she's not willing to help and thinks of it as just another technique, she's apt to say, "The hell with it!"

MRS. RICHTER: Can a couple really create the aura you create in therapy after reading *Human Sexual Inadequacy?*

MRS. JOHNSON: We've worked terribly hard not to make therapy seem to be done by "the numbers." Couples have to approach their problems individually. Two people who want to overcome their difficulties can start, at least in theory, by reading the book carefully.

DR. MASTERS: People who want to correct their dysfunction ought to read the book before going to a counselor. Then, after they have talked with someone they could go back and read again those parts that have special value to them.

MR. BELLIVEAU: Can most couples find adequate help for their sexual problems?

DR. MASTERS: Perhaps fifty percent of people with sexual problems have no authority to go to for help. If they read this book at least they might be helped. Remember that a significant part of sexual dysfunction is caused by lack of information.

MRS. JOHNSON: Our results are beginning to help people, and that is becoming known. That will build acceptance of our methods and lead to more training of various kinds of therapists because the public will demand it. It's getting to the point where medicine is no longer going to be allowed an attitude of neglect anymore about sexual dysfunction.

DR. MASTERS: If our book is read, and your book about our work is read, doctors are going to be busier than ever because people will realize that they do not have to stay dysfunctional. They'll go in for help and force doctors, psychologists, and clergymen to learn something about sexual dysfunction.

MRS. RICHTER: Do you think more knowledge of sex can lead to promiscuity?

MRS. JOHNSON: People have to learn that social control is as compatible with knowledge as much as with sexual myths and distortions. It's absolutely insane to think that knowledge can create promiscuity. If we substitute a genuine value system for one that hasn't worked —that has created sexual dysfunction—we can be rid of fear, disease, and illegitimacy. Knowledge would give us better social control.

MRS. RICHTER: A single sex standard for men and women—will it really work?

DR. MASTERS: The only aspect of my field that I am really belligerent toward is the double standard. A single standard of sexual behavior for everyone is the only avenue to satisfying sexual functioning for everyone. However, I am not so sure we are moving toward the single standard.

MRS. JOHNSON: The double standard is perpetuated by both sexes. People who don't really want to be responsible for their behavior are the ones who hide behind the double standard.

DR. MASTERS: Women are not always ready to accept a single standard either. They still want their own set of privileges. Our culture today is trying to give the female all of the male advantages without the disadvantages. I am opposed to that.

MRS. JOHNSON: The woman who wants equal privilege cannot have it without responsibility.

DR. MASTERS: I couldn't agree with you more.

MR. BELLIVEAU: What about your failures with patients?

DR. MASTERS: When we fail it is our responsibility. A lot of people come here and think this is a mecca. Obviously it is not. When people leave here with their problems unsolved, we stress that *we* failed—they did not. We suggest other forms of psychotherapy that may be better suited to them.

MR. BELLIVEAU: Are you being modest in reporting your statistics as "failure rates" rather than "success rates"?

DR. MASTERS: The issue involved is very simple. If you start talking about success, particularly with something of a behavioral nature, you must define success. What is success? No matter what you read, each scientific investigator has a somewhat different criterion. But if you report that you have a failure almost everybody understands what you are talking about.

MRS. RICHTER: Do you plan to teach your techniques to other therapists?

MRS. JOHNSON: We would like to have four or five therapy teams as a permanent part of the Foundation staff, but certainly no more. We now have one other team, as you know—Dr. Schumacher and Dr. Spitz. They are very good and have learned our techniques well, and we've learned from them too. It works both ways.

MRS. RICHTER: Do many professionals ask to come for training?

DR. MASTERS: During the past ten years, word of our therapy program has spread throughout the world, and rarely does a day go by that we don't receive a request for information or an application for training from someone either here or abroad. We have 200 applications from well-prepared, serious dual-sex teams who would like to train with us, and we hope to start a postgraduate program with a few teams at a time, starting in the fall of 1970. We'll train these teams so that they can return home and teach other teams, but just how long our training program will be we do not know yet.

Recently we made an arrangement with the medical school at Washington University for selected senior medical students to spend three months at the Foundation, and starting July, 1970, senior residents from the department of urology began taking part of their training with us.

MRS. JOHNSON: We think that ultimately we can do a better job being free of routine therapy so that we can teach others. I think I could train someone to be a better therapist than I am.

MR. BELLIVEAU: How do you feel about the recognition you have had so far?

DR. MASTERS: Well, there has been a lot of negative and a lot of positive feeling about us. Plenty of people opposed to us are at least having to think. People are beginning to be aware that there is a need in this area.

MR. BELLIVEAU: Do you think your contributions in sexology have helped shape the times?

MRS. JOHNSON: We emerged with the times. I believe we draw from the signals that are going on around us. If you play the game of signals, you respond to them.

Bill and I are alike in that we are both people who look for signals. You emerge into new directions that way. Bill obviously grew up not liking the mundane; he was never interested in the thing that just anybody could do. But once having emerged, yes, we have shaped the times.

DR. MASTERS: It is interesting to see how different the times are now compared to the period just after publication of *Human Sexual Response*. Since publication of *Human Sexual Inadequacy* we have received practically no hate mail and very little opposition from any quarter. There is definitely a more accepting climate now, but I don't mean to imply that we are completely accepted, even today. Kinsey did open up the field considerably in recent times, but the prior men, Van de Velde and Dickinson, didn't even venture into sex research until they were over sixty-five and retired. Their times just wouldn't allow it. This just isn't an attractive field for original investigators. There is a lot of social pressure against you and there are few financial rewards. Ask most doctors if they would give up their practices to go into sex research and see what they would say.

MRS. JOHNSON: We really want to see people do more work, but no one now is going to risk his reputation and income to work in a field that is still unacceptable to much of society, unless he or she is professionally secure or a crusader type.

MRS. RICHTER: Dr. Masters, do you think you would ever retire from the Foundation?

DR. MASTERS: I would only retire if someone came to me and said, "Here's enough money to equip a neurophysiology laboratory—Now go ahead and work." The thing I most want to do is be part of a neurology lab so I can figure out how people have orgasm and what makes them ejaculate. If I had support for ten years and could work in the lab some really incredible stuff might develop in terms of human sexual function at the basic science level that everyone could apply.

MR. BELLIVEAU: You really feel that the laboratory is going to offer some important answers?

DR. MASTERS: I'd love to come up with a report that no one could read, except specialists in the field. If I could get the neurophysiology of ejaculation and orgasm worked out it would be the greatest contribution I could make. Also, no one knows anything about cardio-respiratory physiology as it relates to sexual functioning. How many times have we heard of the doctor who tells a cardiac patient to take it easy when he's asked about frequency of intercourse. The doctor doesn't have any answers because nothing is known about this subject. Most universities won't allow sex research so it will undoubtedly be some time before we have real answers.

MRS. RICHTER: Do you see your techniques being changed, or bastardized in the future? Would it matter to you? Freud, for example, came along and set out certain theories that were eventually challenged and modified. If this were done with your techniques, would that bother you?

DR. MASTERS: All I can say is that we won't have Freud's disadvantage. We have not dealt with theory. With Freud's death, his theories were accepted as "the word"—that is the worst kind of thing that could happen. We would never want our laboratory findings or therapy techniques accepted in this way.

MRS. JOHNSON: We have written in the preface to *Human Sexual Inadequacy* that it is our expectation that the book will be obsolete in the next decade.

DR. MASTERS: I expect that a lot of people are going

to come up with ways of bettering what we have done. As more and more people work with our techniques there are bound to be variations—some good and some bad.

MRS. JOHNSON: We would like to think that the book has a message of hope. If *Human Sexual Inadequacy* is accepted, and if people reach for it and it makes things work better for them, they will begin thinking about themselves as naturally sexual individuals. Then they won't need us. We don't care if our techniques are obsolete ten years from now. If they are, that would be wonderful because it would mean significant progress has been made. If progress has been made, that is a contribution, and as far as we are concerned this is what matters.